MY THIRTY YEARS' WAR

By Margaret Anderson

MY THIRTY YEARS' WAR
THE FIERY FOUNTAINS
THE LITTLE REVIEW ANTHOLOGY
THE UNKNOWABLE GURDJIEFF
THE STRANGE NECESSITY

MARGARET C. ANDERSON

My Thirty Years' War

THE AUTOBIOGRAPHY

beginnings and battles to 1930

HORIZON PRESS   NEW YORK

CONTENTS

PREFACE

If I were asked to express in a phrase the emotion that has most often recurred during my lifetime, day after day, I would answer: the emotion that I can never be thankful enough for all that life has given me. And I would add that, without any Faustian bargaining on my part, it has given me everything that I consider worth dying for.

Thus I feel that I have *found,* without having had to *seek.*

A friend once said to me, "You are the only really happy person I have ever known". And another friend asked, "Have you ever felt like Atlas?" NO, I said, if you mean in the sense of carrying a weight, a burden, on my shoulders. YES, in the sense that I've been carrying the heavens — for the benefit of my own, and other, lives. You understand that I think life has been too kind to me, has spared me any real burdens: even my losses, through death, have been transmutations.

Therefore, at the beginning of my life's end, I have no further wishes. I have seen all the places I wanted to see, done all the things I wanted to do, heard all the music I longed to hear, made all the friends one dares to hope for, and found love that is beyond all hope. These blessings have been bestowed upon me in spite of my shortcomings and my lack of equipment for an adult life; leaving me with remorse for things left undone, for things only half understood, for knowledge never acquired, for efforts never made; but with a provision for "those zones of old pain where one may rest".

In this book I have told the beginning of my happy lifestory. In a second volume. *The Fiery Fountains,* published in 1951, I continued with the happiness and the inevitable appearance of the first great sorrows. The third volume, *The Strange Necessity,* to be published in 1969, brings the story up to date.

Sometimes I feel like the soldier who, shamed at not having been wounded in the war, always limped when walking past his wounded comrades. Such is my feeling of guilt at having been spared so much of the suffering of the world.

Le Cannet, France
May, 1969

to

Georgette Leblanc

> . . . the only human being
> I have known who has none
> of the human *bêtises* . . .

MY THIRTY YEARS' WAR

MY THIRTY YEARS' WAR

My greatest enemy is reality.
I have fought it successfully for thirty years.

What have I been so unreal about? I have never been able to accept the two great laws of humanity—that you're always being suppressed if you're inspired and always being pushed into the corner if you're exceptional. I won't be cornered and I won't stay suppressed. This book is a record of these refusals.

It isn't that I'm aggressive. But life is antagonistic. You spend a few years fighting your family because they want you to be what you don't want to be—mine wanted me to be Aimée McPherson. You make friends who love your ideas and lose them because they don't know what an idea is. You fight the mob because it wants to make you or break you. You fall in love, and you soon find out what that is—giving to one human being the opportunity to invade and misunderstand you that you wouldn't dream of giving to the mob.

So then you fight the individual. And finally you find your stride . . . and from then on everything goes just as badly as ever. So then you fight the whole system again from the beginning.

My unreality is chiefly this: I have never felt much like a human being. It's a splendid feeling.

I have no place in the world—no fixed position. I don't know just what kind of thing I am. Nobody else seems to know either. I appear to be a fairly attractive woman in her thirties. But such a human being falls inevitably into one or more of the human categories—is someone's daughter, sister, niece, aunt, wife, mistress or mother. I am not a daughter: my father is dead and my mother rejected me long ago. I am not a sister: my two sisters find me more than a little mad, and that is no basis for a sisterly relationship. I am certainly not a niece; it was my aunt who held out for Aimée McPherson and we haven't spoken since. I could almost be called an aunt (no one would dare), but my two nephews don't find me convincing; so I'm not an aunt. I am no man's wife, no man's delightful mistress, and I will never, never, never be a mother.

I look like various things, at various seasons: like the Ritz in the winter (if my tailor has done well by my shoulders); like a musical comedy in the summer—or rather like something in those old operettas—"Robin Hood" perhaps; also like a tennis player, a sailor, or a great deal like Little Lord Fauntleroy. In the late fall I look like the Dame aux Camelias. In the early spring I look as if the world were mine.

And I never have a cent—in any season.

I can't earn my own living. I could never make anything turn into money. It's like making fires. A careful assortment of paper, shavings, faggots and kindling nicely tipped with pitch will never light for me. I have never been present when a cigarette butt, extinct, thrown into a damp and isolated spot, started a conflagration in the California woods. But then there are so many natural laws that I don't understand. I never see them working.

I have always held myself quite definitely aloof from natural laws. . . .

My first fight—the first I remember—was when I was five or six. It was a question of handwriting. I was engaged in making large round letters on a piece of paper—perfectly uniform but perfectly ugly.

I considered them good-looking and felt the necessity to tell my aunt I would always write like that. She said it was probable I would change my style before I was twenty, as nearly everyone did. I said that wasn't a good reason, that I wouldn't change mine. She said it was natural to change.

I said I loved my handwriting. I said (in my own little way) that that was enough to preserve it against the onslaughts of time and nature. She said I was talking foolishly. I said I couldn't see any reason in her argument, but that mine was solid. I thought my handwriting was beautiful, if she wanted the truth, and that was a good reason why I wouldn't change it. (I was glad to make a conversation in which I could use the word beautiful.)

She said I might change my idea of beautiful. And this made me so angry that I didn't sleep all night. I kept trying

5

to find an argument on the theme that beauty does not change.

At breakfast I announced that I wasn't like other people; that I loved my handwriting more than they loved theirs and that if it were beautiful now it would necessarily be beautiful when I was twenty. Or, if I were weak enough to change, and my later style were also beautiful, that wouldn't affect the fact that the first was beautiful. Two beautiful things.

You may be right, said my aunt who was worn out. She thought I looked ill and asked me if I had a fever.

I said no, if she could follow my argument I would be all right. And I thought I had too many good ideas on questions like these to be treated like a baby.

Next I remember telling my mother that ball was spelled with an "o." She insisted it was "a." I couldn't accept this and it didn't occur to me that she might have some authority on her side; it had to be "o" because of the sound. My conviction was so intense that I began to have a fearful pain in the heart. I thought I was going to choke or faint. To relieve this feeling I began to cry and shake my fists at the ceiling. Finally mother showed me in the dictionary that she was right. For hours afterward I was so depressed that everyone was frightened. I couldn't very well explain, but I felt a resentment against God or man for having imposed an incredible stupidity upon the world. And the world had accepted it. . . .

6

I will now rush into adolescence—you can't be any more bored with childhood stories than I am. Still I have had to show what a boring person I was, because I was just as boring as this when I started the *Little Review*.

*   *   *   *   *   *

I liked my home and disliked my family. I should say I disliked families and liked my homes, for we had a new home every year. Mother had a passion for houses, furniture, interior decoration, and the only way to satisfy this was to move as often as possible. Dad always consented on condition that she retain at least some of the old furniture. But she always broke her promises, and every new year found us installed in a new house with new color schemes, new carpets, curtains, lamps and, naturally, new furniture.

We were living in Columbus, Indiana, when I finally managed to escape the reality of family life. I was just out of college. College had been wonderful for me—wonderfully unreal: three years of escape from authority, duty, regulations, bells and gongs, study and of course knowledge. And finally an escape from the fourth year. I remember only moonlight nights on balconies, violet-hunts in the spring, the smell of autumn orchards from class-room windows, walks in the snow to a farmhouse for fudge, dances arranged as an evasion of study, long evenings of reading books that were not in the curriculum, nights of cramming for exams and passing, with high marks, subjects about which I knew nothing. The

7

only piece of exact knowledge I have retained—heaven knows why—is the law of Archimedes. I can still say it: A body immersed in a liquid is buoyed up by a force equal to the weight of the water displaced by it. I suppose I sensed in this a promise of escape from a *very* disagreeable reality.

Chiefly college meant one thing to me: pianos. My course was so arranged, by special permission, that I escaped Greek in order to study the piano. Not that I studied it. But I played it. I never learned any piece of music completely because there was always some passage in it that displeased me and this I refused to examine. Principally, I made other people play the piano for me.

There were three or four girls, advanced pupils, who played extremely well. One of them beautifully. I spent my time listening to them, pointing out what I would do instead of what they were doing, dictating, criticizing, rehearsing, conducting, gasping, ecstasying. The absurd part of it was that they were all much older than I and possessed all the musical knowledge I lacked—because I had ecstasied from the age of six instead of learning anything. Even my music teachers played to me instead of making me play to them. Once when I was seriously ill the current music teacher was engaged to play for me a whole day. She seemed to like it.

The girl who played beautifully had a balcony. She allowed me to sit there rapturously on spring nights and be played to for hours. Her name was Bina McKibbon—even a layman should have refused such a name. I christened her Elizabeth. . . . All my life I shall remember those Bach-Beethoven-Brahms-Schumann-Chopin nights under the stars and the elms of Western College, Oxford, Ohio, between Dayton and Cincinnati and conveniently near Indianapolis where my hopeful family waited for me to finish my education and come home to the higher joys of country clubs and bridge.

Not that I didn't like country clubs. I even liked bridge. It was a game to be fought and won. I liked golf and the hot and cold showers and the chicken and waffles on the club porch afterward. But I really couldn't see this as my life, which was to be beautiful as no life had ever been.

*   *   *   *   *   *

Mother was a nervous woman. There is no more charming classification if you're nervous on purpose, but when you're nervous because you can't help it there is nothing more trying. Mother couldn't help it, didn't want to help it—in fact, her attitude was a positive one. She liked being a victim of nerves because it made everything disagreeable, and she was one of those persons who gets an infinite pleasure out of making things disagreeable. I hope she won't be hurt in case she reads this book. I have told her all this in the most courteous and analytical terms but she never found anything to say except that I was crazy. Well, that was her opinion. My opinion is that she was nervous. It's important to have a free exchange of opinion in the family. It will get you absolutely nowhere. Still, opinion

9

for opinion's sake—opinion for God's sake, I have always held.

Mother could fill the house with those vibrations that penetrate every wall, even if you were reading with concentration in the attic. In fact reading was one of the activities that most irritated her. Not that she didn't love to read. Nothing delighted her more than a sincerely mediocre book. But my reading was likely to be of an improving nature—Ellen Key, Havelock Ellis, Dostoievsky—or of a poetical nature—Shelley, Keats, Swinburne; and it was this she didn't like. She suspected it of making me discontented. She never suspected, as the fairy tales so prettily teach, that the Blue Bird of discontent is not to be searched afar but to be found right in the home.

Mother was always telling me that I could be Ella Wheeler Wilcox if I would only improve my mind and morals and that I could easily be Fanny Bloomfield-Zeisler if I would only practice the piano a little. But every time she saw me with a book she made a scene about people who waste their time reading. And every time I approached the piano she made a scene about people who waste their time working instead of being "social." She wanted me to be social with her friends. I was—with the result they liked to come and talk with me rather than with her. She asked three of her best friends never to come again—that I wasted too much time being social.

Dad was a poignant man. He talked like Lincoln, looked like Forbes Robertson and I always felt he was thinking, "The rest is silence."

. . . Columbus, Indiana. Just out of college.

I had a green room overlooking lilac bushes, yellow roses and oak trees. Every day I shut myself in, planning how to escape mediocrity (not the lilacs and roses but the vapidities that went on in their hearing).

Escape and conquer the world.

I already knew that the great thing to learn about life is, first, not to do what you don't want to do, and, second, to do what you do want to do.

I invaded dad's business offices, learned to use the type-writer, then came back to the green room and wrote twenty-page typed letters to him, exposing the criminality of our family life and offering a program upon which he could act in every domestic crisis. These letters I placed on his desk so that they would have the first claim on his attention in the morning.

After the first two he said nothing, hoping I had written myself out. After the third he came home with a sad face. He took me aside and said he'd read my letter carefully and that it seemed to him extremely bitter; that he had no idea I felt that way about things. I answered that I supposed he felt much the same way. He confessed he hated living as we did; if he could do as he liked he would lead a simple life in the woods or read or travel. I am sure nothing could have been more odious to him than producing money for four extravagant women (I have two charming sisters: Lois, the family humorist, and Jean whom everyone called the Venus de Milo. They called me the Victory, which gave me a great deal—but, to me, not too much—to live up to) to spend on their looks—or their houses. So I asked him why he didn't do something to change it all and he said it was too late.

At this point mother came downstairs. As usual dad looked quickly at her face to gauge her mood. When she was particularly nervous he became conciliating. When she was happily playing the martyr he became soothing. When she was merely unpleasant he began a series of amusing stories.

His attitude always made me weak with fury. I wanted him to fight.

*   *   *   *   *   *

We subscribed to all the more obnoxious magazines— the *Ladies' Home Journal* and another in the same category called *Good Housekeeping*. One day in this I noticed a department conducted by Clara E. Laughlin (of the So You're Going to Paris? Series)—a department of advice to young girls. The advice seemed to prescribe none of the immobility usually urged upon the young, so I decided to ask Miss Laughlin how a perfectly nice but revolting girl could leave home. My letter was long (I was always long); I listed everything I found immoral in the family situation and asked her if she considered me crazy. She answered by return post that I didn't seem at all crazy, that my letter was the most interesting she had received —had I read Edward Gosse's "Father and Son," and wouldn't I come to Chicago to talk with her?

What could I possibly want to talk about, asked the

family. About my life, naturally. Wasn't my life an envi-
able one—hadn't I everything I wanted? Yes, materially.
What else did I want? Self-expression. What was that?
asked dad. Mother looked sarcastic. I said it was being
able to think, say and do what you believed in.

Seems to me you do nothing else, said dad.

But I went. Dad took me.

*   *   *   *   *   *

Chicago: enchanted ground to me from the moment
Lake Michigan entered the train windows. I would make
my beautiful life here. A city without a lake wouldn't
have done.

As usual I felt I had only to decide something and it
would happen. I have a single superstition—that the gods
are for me and that anything I want will happen if I
play at it hard enough. I can't say work at it because anything I work at never seems to come out right. I never
could have talked French if I had worked at it. I just
wanted to talk, felt impelled to talk and in three weeks I
was talking. That's really all I know about it. Of course
I don't talk beautiful French, but why should I have tried
to? Only a few French people talk beautiful French. I
talk a fantastic, amusing and invented language that gives
more pleasure to the French than grammar could possibly give. It's all in one's conception of things; I'd rather
entertain people than not. And I'd rather entertain myself
thinking up curious ways to say difficult things than bore
myself studying how to say what everyone else is saying

13

and saying it in the same way. Of course I do put a certain effort into achieving the difference. But then any language deserves this much consideration from any one. . . .

*　　*　　*　　*　　*　　*

Michigan Boulevard had a smell of water across its asphalt and a soft gray light over its shops. The doorman at the Annex—black, white-gloved, white-toothed—was resplendent in red, blue and gold and almost hysterical in his efforts to make you like his hotel. I went at once into the flower shop and had white lilacs sent up to my room. I put them against the lake which became more blue than it has ever been since.

Dad and I dined and went to the theatre—John Barrymore in "The Stubborn Cinderella," which was on for a summer run. This was dad's choice. I would have chosen something "serious." But it didn't matter; I was too busy thinking of other things; chiefly of that triumphant life which was to begin in Chicago.

Back in my hotel room I could hear the beat of the orchestras where I sat by the lilacs looking out at the lake. There was a lighthouse that sent its searchlight hypnotically into my window. I began to repeat a vow to the rhythm of the light: I will become something beautiful. I swear it. . . .

*　　*　　*　　*　　*　　*

The next day at eleven I went to Clara Laughlin's office in Randolph Street. She was the literary editor of a religious weekly called the *Interior*, financed by Cyrus Mc-Cormick. Her affiliations with it were social rather than religious, for she knew everyone and was invaluable for literary gossip.

I loved the section of Randolph and Clark Streets—dark, high, depressing. I went up a stairway and was shown into an office where a stout, vigorous and smiling woman waited to receive me. She looked like Melba. She seemed surprised by me—agreeably, may I say without vanity. It would be unbecoming of me not to know that I was extravagantly pretty in those days—extravagantly and disgustingly pretty. I looked like a composite of all the most offensive magazine covers.

We began to talk and talked so long that we were nearly excluded from Plows for luncheon. At tea time we went back to the Annex where dad presented himself to Miss Laughlin, expressed the hope that my self-expression wouldn't submerge her, and then left for Columbus. She and I talked on until dinner. I remember we dined hurriedly on a salad of alligator pears, which she recommended highly and which I highly disliked. Alligator pears have always remained for me a superfluous food which one consumes when one has no need of food at all, being so completely nourished by one's emotions.

Miss Laughlin went out to her home on the North Side to fetch the manuscript of a play she was writing and joined me for the theatre. I had chosen Eugene Walter's "The Easiest Way," with Frances Starr, which was making rather a sensation in Chicago at the moment. It seemed a good enough play to me—except for the title which certainly should have been "The Hardest Way."

Afterward in the Annex the orchestras filled my room again while Clara Laughlin read me a sentimental play on which Belasco had already paid her an enormous advance—one of those plays that never gets put on (one wonders why, Belasco loving sentimentality as he does). But my evening wasn't ruined. I was hearing a real author read a real play, which was certainly better than sitting in Columbus, Indiana, writing letters. (Why on earth should I have thought so?) Anyway, I was enchanted and when Miss Laughlin left I spent the night thinking of all the people I'd been hearing about—people she knew and whom I wanted to know: Ellen Terry, Irving, Barrie, the Barrymores (especially Maurice, who used to come to her office, sometimes looking like Beau Brummel, sometimes like a tramp); Mansfield, Richard Harding Davis, Booth Tarkington, James Whitcomb Riley, Theodore Thomas, Fanny Bloomfield-Zeisler (with whom Miss Laughlin went to concerts, Mrs. Zeisler always lamenting that her critical faculty never permitted her the simple pleasure of listening to music emotionally); Maude Adams, Mrs. Fisk, Julia Marlowe, Charles Frohman, Frances Starr. All her stories about these people were human, witty, charming. Here was an atmosphere in which I could live and breathe. I saw no reason why I should continue to live in Columbus, Indiana, and not breathe.

The next morning at eleven I went again to Randolph Street. I was to leave for home on a noon train, and let my hansom cab wait while I went up to say good-by. I hadn't planned even to sit down. But I had so much to talk about that I didn't have time to sit down. I stood by Miss Laughlin's desk and began all over again. At two o'clock I was still standing there; we had forgotten the train. I had a five dollar cab bill to pay.

We took the tired hansom back to the Annex, lunched and talked, teaed and talked, dined and talked, went to another play and talked. I said good-by, made more vows to the lighthouse and the next morning sent her dozens of pink roses—pink being her favorite. I was critical of this and almost sent yellow instead. Still, I decided, people should sometimes be allowed to have what they want. . . .

When I arrived in Columbus I was babbling with enthusiasm. Mother had always said that my enthusiasm on any subject sickened her; she seemed now ready to die of nausea.

The next day brought a special delivery letter from Clara Laughlin to the family. I was an unusually interesting girl, I should be given an opportunity. She would be glad to take me under her wing (yes, wing). I had read more than anyone of my age she'd ever known, I should now begin to know life. For a start she could arrange for me to do interviews with stage celebrities. I could earn enough money to be independent.

Then came days of trouble. I fought not only for my right to go but for every abstract right for anyone to do anything. I locked myself in my green room, searched my brain for inspired arguments, issued forth and delivered them in the living room as before an assembled multitude. The arguments were always long. Sometimes I had such a choice and complicated bit of thinking that I had to put it on paper. I made carbon copies of everything—one for mother, one for dad, one for Lois and Jean. I felt my growing sisters should know about the cerebrality that was going on, since I was doing all their fighting for them. Besides I sometimes distrusted their pitying glances. Lois called me Elsie Dinsmore. Why do you care whether they understand anything or not? she asked in astonishment. The thing to do is to go. Don't be so polite to them and don't try to reform them.

Lois was so flippant and I so loquacious that mother spent her time telephoning to dad's office during important directors' meetings, urging him to come home and deal with his unnatural daughter—singular, and meaning me.

Finally, out of boredom, I think, they let me go.

* * * * * *

Chicago. November. . . .

Lois went with me. Not that she particularly wanted to go, but the weary family preferred it. I couldn't see what she was getting out of it, going anywhere without convictions.

From the train we hurried to Orchestra Hall for our first Chicago Symphony concert (Frederick Stock conducting), and I knew that I was the happiest person in the world. We were there early, bought twenty-five cent seats, ran without stopping up the hundred and ten steps to the gallery and were seated in the front row in time to hear the tuning up. Bruno Steindal, first 'cellist, was soloist and played the Bach Air on the G string. When the first strains came floating up to the heaven of the gallery I put my head on the railing and wept as one only weeps a few times in one's life.

Two afternoons later (Sunday) after standing before the Venus in the Art Institute, we went across the street to heaven again where Gadski was giving a concert. It was the fashion in those days to spread a long, wide, white strip of canvas from the stage door, where the artist entered, to the piano, where it terminated in a large square. This was to protect her long and trailing gown. She stood upon the square of white in the curve of the black piano— a modern effect and very fine. Sembrich, I remember, on leaving the stage always ran the last three or four steps to the door coquettishly with her breast held up rigidly like a pigeon in the best stout prima donna tradition. Gadski always walked the entire length majestically. On this particular and divine occasion Frank Lafargue was her accompanist—I could find no fault with him—and she sang as an opening number Brahms' *A Thought Like Music*. In all the thousands of concert programs I have heard in the years since not one has ever featured this lovely song. From our front row (where we sat all winter, making touching vows to each other never to come alone since, in case of fire, we preferred to be burned together)

19

I formed a way of half closing my eyes until everything in the hall became blurred except the singer and the piano. The optical illusion produced a cubist canvas. She stood in a circle of light in which was contained the square of canvas and the planes of the black piano. The music was sharper, more unbearable, like this. . . .

The next day at noon, walking on Michigan Boulevard, I saw Gadski approaching. I must have looked radiant at seeing her, for she smiled at me, stopped, took my hand and walked on.

*   *   *   *   *   *

It had been agreed that we would live simply, unextravagantly, in Chicago, pretending to be poor art students beginning our careers. Lois was to study the pipe organ and I interviewing. We had gone to an institution known as the Y. W. C. A. Clara Laughlin had an aunt who was an official there and they felt it would be wise for us to live under the protection of Christianity. It smelled (the institution—also the Christianity) like a laundry. But neither Lois nor I minded. We thought it interesting. The bad food, the unattractive people, the uncomfortable beds, the sap-green walls of our room faded before the fact that the building was on Michigan Boulevard, two blocks from the Annex, four blocks from Orchestra Hall and the Art Institute; and I could see the same lighthouse from our window.

Our first unextravagant gesture was to rent a piano from Steinway and Company—a simple upright, but costly beyond the ambitions of art students. My next was to present myself at Clara Laughlin's office which had conveniently moved to Wabash Avenue just back of the Annex.

No stage celebrities were in town at the moment, so she asked me if I had ever reviewed books. Naturally not. Would I like to? Naturally. Did I know how to go about it? Not at all. But I had read lots of them and if she would criticize my first effort I was sure I could learn. I needn't worry, she said, she had broken in any number of good reviewers. My first effort would probably be bad but she would be ruthlessly frank. She gave me Stephen Phillips' "Herod."

I had read his "Marpessa" (and am sorry to say thought it excellent). I read "Herod" carefully that afternoon and spent the next morning carefully reviewing it. The care was to assemble every platitude that has ever been incorporated in a book review. Of the two I liked "Marpessa" better, so I talked rather of it than of "Herod." I couldn't help feeling that I was rather good—that is, I thought the platitudes good, but I couldn't imagine how I had got to know them all. It sounded learned. Still, I was a little unconfident and hadn't the courage to present myself with the review and wait for the ruthless frankness. I sent it by messenger and followed an hour later.

Clara Laughlin's face was beaming and tender when I went in.

But, my dear, I haven't a word to say, not a word to blue-pencil. No one ever sent me in a first review like this. It's perfect. I might have written it myself. You can take all the books you want.

Which only shows what platitudes will do for you.

*   *   *   *   *   *

In those days books were published at lower prices. All novels sold for a dollar and a half. When you finished reviewing them you took them to McClurg's and sold them for seventy-five cents each. This was your salary.

I began reviewing too for the *Chicago Evening Post*. Francis Hackett was literary editor and had already gained the reputation of publishing the livest book page in the middle west. One day after I had been reviewing for him for perhaps two weeks, Francis wrote me a letter.

Why all the big words? I have to cut half of them out. A little simplicity, please, and at intervals a great word for beauty.

I tried, but I was too proud of my vocabulary and my clichés to renounce them suddenly. When I finally woke to the horror of what I was doing I made such an effort to be simple that I lost my vocabulary forever.

Sometimes Clara Laughlin would telephone me on Saturday morning.

I've fifty books that must be reviewed by Monday. Can you do it?

Naturally.

And I never missed the Chicago Symphony on Saturday night nor the Sunday afternoon concert. Monday morning the reviews were always ready.

Everything should have gone well for us in Chicago. Everything did except money. At home we had been given allowances for some time—Lois and I each fifty dollars a month and Jean thirty. This was to provide us with small necessary luxuries and to train us to spend money sensibly. I had always spent mine for flowers, books and music for people who charmed me. I remember the inscription dad wrote in the account books when he first gave them to us:

> If I thought that money made for happiness I could wish that this were more. But since I know it does not, I can only wish you more of happiness.

Our methods of expenditure hadn't trained us to cope with the economic situation of art students. We impressively opened a charge account at Fleming H. Revell's and bought four oriental rugs to redeem our hideous room. Lois had a passion for travel and luggage and was always having fitted bags delivered from Marshall Field's —just when we had decided never to travel again. Of course we had to buy most of the charming clothes we saw; and I was so optimistic about my book sales that I indulged in a yellow rose every day. We depleted the candy shop of the Y and developed a taste for smoking. We initiated our friends of the Y, and from then on supplied their cigarettes as well as our own. There was one art student with no money at all, and as we were convinced that she was a genius (she had been discovered

23

weeping before a statue in the Art Institute) of course we had to give her as much money as possible.

We would finally have emerged from our strained financial situation with honor and credit, I am sure (I always have), but Clara Laughlin heard of the cigarettes and the debts, thought we were going to the dogs and wrote an hysterical letter to the family which brought mother and dad to the Annex by the first train. We were melodramatically sent for. Lois was accused of things she had never dreamed of doing and it was decided to take us both home immediately. My career was to be ruined— and I was charged with nothing more criminal than the daily rose. I argued brilliantly but everyone was worn out with the emotionality expended on us (and on a lot of very loose thinking) and didn't care to listen. Clara Laughlin found a moment to announce that one of her best friends had died that morning and this in some way seemed to double our crimes.

The affair of the cigarettes constituted the great scandal. (This was in 1912.)

Dad took us back to the Y at midnight. We had refused to stay at the Annex. We walked along Michigan Boulevard silently. I was certain that the time had come for suicide. To leave the Chicago Orchestra—I couldn't think beyond this.

At the door of the Y I found my voice.

I cannot and will not go home with mother. I can't get back into her atmosphere.

Go to sleep and don't think about it any more. Your

mother will take the morning train. We'll go in the afternoon.

That night—I don't want to think of it even now.

The next afternoon in the chair car I offered a few calm
statements on the injustice of the situation.

Don't get excited, said dad. I imagine those two women
were a little hysterical.

He took a cigar from his pocket and started toward the
smoker. Then he hesitated and turned back, smiling.

Will you join me? he asked.

*　　*　　*　　*　　*　　*

This was in April. I determined to be back in Chicago
by June.

A great abyss opened in our house. Lois and I had made
a pact to ignore mother's taunts, threats, misinterpretations and revilings. There should be silence and calm.
Dad was always charming with us but he would never
take a decisive stand against mother's attitude; so we
were forced to abandon him to her. We called the household The Great Divide (William Vaughn Moody's play
of that name had just had a success in Chicago).

After a week of the silence mother decided to travel.
We were left in charge of a family friend whom we had
always called chaperone. She came to live with us. She
was acceptable—she knew both Chicago and New York.

For four days I talked to her of what Chicago meant to
me, how I meant to get back and of what revenge would
be appropriate for Clara Laughlin. Finally, I found it. I

would write her a letter. In all the great crises of my life there seems never to have been between me and the up-heavals of the universe any resource but a scrap of paper.

I wrote a magistral epistle, telling Miss Laughlin how misguided she had been and announcing that I was com-ing back. She answered that it might be a good idea for me to come alone. Also that I could always count on books to review.

So I made my plans. There is no use saying that I worked over them. I didn't. I had no money, for our allowances had been stopped at mother's suggestion. But I needed only railroad fare, as I meant to get a job in Chi-cago and never take another cent from home. I sold my calf-skin Ibsen and two exquisite silk negligées—and thought no more about money.

We were happy, since mother was away, and spent the time as we always did when we were alone—making music. We had a six-piece orchestra—that is, I played the piano and whistled, Jean sang soprano and played the banjo, Lois sang alto and played tenor on the mandolin. We spent days in the music room, the chaperone as audience.

The Chicago Symphony came to Indianapolis. One would have thought we were its board of promoters, so violent was our proprietorship. We launched into a cam-paign to force all Indianapolis to attend.

Then mother came home. I talked to dad in his office.

26

All right, try it, he said. If you think you have the guts to get on alone in Chicago it may be good for you.

Lois suddenly didn't in the least mind being left behind. She had just fallen in love. He recited so much Swinburne to her that Chicago had already begun to seem a little vulgar. . . .

*   *   *   *   *   *

It being June and the music season over, I went directly to the Y where I took a cheaper room—without the lake and the lighthouse. Then the necessary accident happened—within two days I found a job. I became a book clerk. At eight dollars a week.

Not so bad as it seems. Chicago had a unique bookshop. In the Fine Arts Building, Michigan Boulevard, Frank Lloyd Wright (the architect known for his construction of Japanese houses in America and million-dollar American hotels in Japan) had built the most beautiful bookshop in the world. The walls were rough cement, sand color; the bookshelves, shoulder high, were in the form of stalls, each containing a long reading table and easy chairs. This was on the seventh floor of the building, looking into the lake at one end and, at the other, into the shaded Italian inner court from which tinkled always the sound of pianos . . . and a fountain. Still I'm not sure about the fountain. I have remembered a fountain. There may not have been one.

An L of the shop with a higher ceiling—long, dark, reposing, with an enormous fireplace and great armchairs

27

—housed the rare bindings. Here tea was served and everyone was very smart. All Chicago society came to Browne's Bookstore.

The fine-binding room gave onto the offices of the *Dial,* a literary review founded by Edgar Allan Poe, which at this time was edited by Francis F. Browne. His two sons were associated with him and also directed the bookshop, which was under the financial patronage of Mrs. Cooney Ward and Mrs. Wilmarth. I was soon taken on the staff of the *Dial* and initiated into the secrets of the printing room—composition (monotype and linotype), proofreading, make-up. This practical knowledge was indispensable when I began the *Little Review.*

It all happened by the grace of poetry. Francis Browne knew by heart all the lyric poetry of the world. He and John Burroughs and John Muir spent summer nights on the peaks of the Rockies, gazing at the stars and saying poems in a sort of memory contest—each having the right to go on until he forgot a line. Mr. Browne, I believe, never stopped before dawn. . . . One day he walked into the bookshop in distress, murmuring Matthew Arnold's "eyes too expressive to be grey, too something to be brown." He had forgotten "lovely" and I supplied it. This made a friendship: I became his chief assistant—chiefly poetic.

But June and July—before the poetry episode—took all my courage. The heat was unimaginable, my living quarters unbearable, clerking unthinkable—my snobbism suffered rather more than I like to admit. The family had just moved to another town into a castle: meaning a marvelous old house of turrets and towers, rambling rooms on different levels, a river, bridges, rose arbors, cypress trees, a hoot owl in the pines at night . . . I could barely resist this. I lived on the photographs Lois sent me. Cartloards of new furniture, a red and white living room, a long blue music room. . . . Quiet and cool and fragrant. Chicago was on fire. Lois came up to visit me for two days. She walked into the bookshop unexpectedly and handed me a yellow rose. . . .

It was the first one I had had during the second descent. I am either profligate—or I can be miserly. I knew if I didn't rush to extremes my heritage would swamp me. So I lived without roses. Out of my eight dollars a week I had to pay five and a half for room and board. Every Saturday I committed my one extravagance: fifty cents for a box of chocolates at Guth's in the Annex. This left two dollars for concerts, laundry, emergencies. Of course I could have bought more and cheaper candy, but the box was handsome and satisfied my hunger for luxury. It was the one link with past glory.

No, there was another. At five-thirty when the bookshop closed I used to walk from the Fine Arts Building through the second floor of the Auditorium Hotel, follow the corridor under Congress Street which led into the Annex and stroll down Peacock Alley to the gorgeous Elizabethan Room. I regarded this as my right: except for its size—it was as big as the New York Central Terminal—it was like home: soft davenports, low lights, rich

29

hangings. I wrote letters here, read and steeped myself in my proper atmosphere before going back to that narrow room so tragically turned away from the lake. . . . The maids who came in to restore order treated me with every consideration; they assumed I was living in the hotel.

I was still reviewing books at intervals for the *Interior* (which had now become the *Continent*) and for the *Post*. But Clara Laughlin wasn't satisfied with this.

You're more immersed in books than ever—bookshop, reviews, the *Dial* and all that poetry.

This with scorn: she cared for poetry less than for any other branch of literature. I never heard her quote a line of any quality. Once she threw at me, "a bunch of hyacinths to feed my soul"—but this was in derision. She thought the poetry good but the idea bad. I thought the idea good but the poetry rotten.

I soon began to see that the breach caused by her first misunderstanding of me was widening into an alarming and fundamental disparity.

Go stand on the bridges and watch life, she said. Feel the story in every poor vagabond you may meet there, in every poor waif of a girl who may be wanting to throw herself into the river.

She loved human interest. So did I; but in great poetry, not in those sentimental human stories she was always writing. I knew I would never know any story but my own. . . .

But I went and stood on the bridge one day—the old Rush Street bridge. I had ecstasies on the way, passing through the wholesale district—smells of spices, chocolates, coffees, teas. By the time I came to the bridge I saw no people at all. I saw only boats and foreign ports.

In late September I had a vacation—spent, naturally, in the castle. Fortified with atmosphere, I went back to the Y—but this time on a train that ran directly to the Chicago Symphony. It was October 16. There I was, first row in the gallery—without Lois but also without thoughts of fire and death. I knew now that nothing could stop my life.

The next summer Clara Laughlin suddenly gave up her position on the *Continent* and proposed me as her successor. Naturally I accepted. First because I could no longer stay on the *Dial*—our poetry society had become too lyrical for Mr. Browne, who one day had been moved to kiss me. He was full of sincere and touching apologies the next day, but I was as sincerely displeased as he was contrite. Second, becoming literary editor of the *Continent* meant going to New York to interview all the publishers about their forthcoming books.

A chance to know New York. I was now planning my career from the viewpoint of a general.

I went to the Holland House which was then the most pleasing of New York hotels, at Fifth Avenue and Thirtieth Street. My room was on the Avenue. (No one will care to hear how I subjected New York to the same minute emotionality I had already expended upon Chicago.) I rode on buses between eight and ten in the morning, saw publishers until noon, lunched with them, interviewed others until four, walked on Fifth Avenue until dinner time and then went to theatres and concerts. Of the publishers I liked best Alfred Harcourt who was at that time restraining himself with difficulty under the conservatism of Henry Holt and Company, and who has since founded the house of Harcourt, Brace.

A week of New York and then to Boston. My first visit in Boston was not to a publisher but to the Mason and Hamlin piano. I went to Beacon Street and asked permission to try every piano in the shop. The office force seemed happy to let me. I explained that I had discovered the Mason and Hamlin to be the best piano in the world and that I meant to play it some day better than anyone. They even took me through their factory. I probably played on a hundred pianos. It was so absorbing trying to find out which one was just a little better than all the others that I almost forgot the publishers.

* * * * * *

Back in Chicago I began a marvelous life as literary editor. And I came to love Chicago as one only loves chosen—or lost—cities.

I knew it in every aspect—dirt, smoke, noise, heat, cold, wind, mist, rain, sleet, snow. I walked on Michigan

Boulevard on winter afternoons when the wind was such a tempest and the snow so icy that ropes were stretched along the buildings to keep pedestrians from falling. Only half a dozen ventured out in a day and they at once sat down like bathers in a high surf. On white misty winter mornings at six o'clock, I used to walk the ten miles from Wilson Avenue to Congress Street for the simple pleasure in the exercise and the hot chocolate at Child's afterward. I was always pretending that I was a poor-working-girl, always forgetting that I was really poor—also a working girl.

. . . And I was in love. My first love—I should say, my first real love. And it was a great love—great in everything including disappointment. But oh, how I was in love. . . .

For a year everything went well on the *Continent,* but inevitably that paper began to suffer under my administration and I to chafe under its restrictions. I made the discovery that what they wanted of me was moral rather than literary judgments. I had made the mistake of writing that Dreiser's "Sister Carrie" was a fine piece of work. This might have passed if I had stipulated that its subject matter was immoral. Since this hadn't occurred to me, letters began to pour in protesting that readers (particularly fathers) had given this fine work to their daughters, whereas I could easily have prevented such catastrophes by warning my clientele that the book was about a girl

33

who went wrong—in which case neither father nor daughter would have read it. I passed from one paroxysm of rage to another. The editor of the *Continent* urged me not to give up my book page but to state facts as they were, which simple process would keep me out of trouble. This sent me from paroxysms into paralysis.

What facts? And what do you mean—as they are?

Very simple, said the simple man. When a book is immoral, say so.

How will I know?

That's one thing that everyone knows, he said kindly.

My paralysis changed to St. Vitus dance. The big book season of the coming autumn was on. The *Continent* was swamped with books which had to be reviewed—my pages had to crowd everything in. One afternoon I reviewed a hundred books in three hours—books I had never seen and of course had no time to read. One glance at the cover notes, another at the style, and I dictated sentence criticisms as follows: The alleged adventures of the supposedly typical American in foreign parts; execrable style but well adapted to family fireside reading.

And to think I was being paid for doing this kind of thing. . . .

THE LITTLE REVIEW

I was now twenty-one. And I felt it was time to confer upon life that inspiration without which life is meaningless.

Often in the night I wake with the sensation that something is wrong, that something must be done to give life form. Sometimes it is merely a matter of changing the furniture in a room. I imagine the whole operation, decide each change with precision, feel suddenly healthy and fall into deep sleep. In the morning I arrange the furniture accordingly, and it's always a great success.

So it was for the *Little Review*. I had been curiously depressed all day. In the night I wakened. First precise thought: I know why I'm depressed—nothing inspired is going on. Second: I demand that life be inspired every moment. Third: the only way to guarantee this is to have inspired conversation every moment. Fourth: most people never get so far as conversation; they haven't the stamina, and there is no time. Fifth: if I had a magazine I could spend my time filling it up with the best conversation the world has to offer. Sixth: marvelous idea—salvation. Seventh: decision to do it. Deep sleep.

In the morning I thought no more about it. I didn't

need to think. To me it was already an accomplished fact. I began announcing to everyone that I was about to publish the most interesting magazine that had ever been launched. They found me vague as to why it was going to be so interesting, nebulous as to how it was going to be published, unconcerned about the necessary money, optimistic about manuscripts. Where any sane person would have explained that, sensing the modern literary movement which was about to declare itself, a review to sponsor it was a logical necessity, I only accused people of being unimaginative because they couldn't follow my élan. They really must be blind! As I remember, I never stated one basic reason why a *Little Review,* devoted to the seven arts, was necessary and inevitable. All this seemed so unimportant compared to the divine afflatus necessary to start it. I never said anything, I believe, except: It will be marvelous. I never say basic things. I forget to. They're so obvious.

I knew that someone would give the money. This is one kind of natural law I always see in operation. Someone would have to. Of course someone did.

During my year as literary editor Floyd Dell had become literary editor of the *Chicago Evening Post*—a position arrived at through an extraordinary article he had written, as a reporter, about the telephone directory. His Friday book section was even more personal and brilliant than Francis Hackett's had been. Floyd's injunctions to his reviewers were invariably interesting: Here is a book on China. Now don't send me an article about China but one about yourself.

Floyd Dell was surrounded by a literary group that gave promise of being the only one of interest in Chicago. I have always felt a horror, a fear and a complete lack of attraction for any group, of any kind, for any purpose. But I was willing sometimes to see this one because Floyd Dell was in it—was it, rather. I liked Floyd—which means I liked his conversation. Liked it enormously. On the *Post* he was chiefly engaged in pointing out to a naïve but willing public the essential differences between Dostoievsky and Kate Douglas Wiggin. In private he would engage you for hours in the most satisfying polemic on the current Browning discussions, trying to discover through what depravity of the public mind Browning had earned the title of philosopher, considering that "the shallow optimism of 'God's in his heaven, all's right with the world' has never been equalled by anyone with a pretension to thinking."

I often dined with the Dells. Mrs. Dell (Margery Currey) had created a sort of salon for Floyd who was so timid he would never have spoken to anyone if she hadn't relieved him of all social responsibility and presented him as an impersonal being whose only function in life was to talk. He used to stand before the fire, looking like Shelley or Keats (why do we always feel they looked alike?) and prove to his dinner guests that democracy and individualism were synonymous terms. Naturally. You can't be of any value to the world (be a good democrat)

37

unless you're a great individual, and you can't be a great individual without being of value to the world.

Other people since famous came to the Floyd Dells: Theodore Dreiser, Sherwood Anderson, John Cowper Powys with his manias of interest and his: How extraordinary! for topics that failed to interest him; critics whose names I have forgotten; also Jerome Blum, George Cram Cook, Susan Glaspell, Edna Kenton, Llewellyn Jones—and Arthur Davidson Ficke who was concerned about English prose.

Do you really know English prose well enough to found a magazine of criticism?

I know great classic and romantic prose and I can sense a great deal about a new prose which is already forming.

Great prose is great prose—one doesn't talk of new prose, said Ficke.

Floyd and I talked of Pater and of living like the hard gem-like flame. Sherwood Anderson used to listen to us in a certain amazement (resembling fear) and indicating clearly that nothing would induce him into such fancy realms. But I liked Sherwood—because he, too, was a talker and of a highly special type. He didn't talk ideas— he told stories. (It sounds bad but the stories were good. So was the telling.) He said to everyone: You don't mind if I use that story you've just told, do you? No one minded. Sherwood's story never bore any relation to the original. He read us the manuscript of "Windy McPherson's Son." Floyd was passionate about it—I, a little less so. It was a new prose but I knew by Sherwood's look that he would do something even better. I asked him to give me an article for the first number of the *Little Review*.

Dreiser never interested me. He is the kind of person to whom I have nothing to say. And of course he had nothing to say to me—he simply twirled his handkerchief . . . I can only talk to people who love talk for its own sake. Sherwood and Floyd would talk to chairs if they had no other audience. But Dreiser was never any good until some exchange of sex magnetism put him at his ease. I was a very unrelaxed person in those days and all my sex manifestations were expended in ideas. But even when I listened to Dreiser in conversation with women with whom he could establish a quick sex sympathy, his talk had no flavor for me. Sex display puts you at your best if you're a tempered human being—becomes responsible for wit. But Dreiser had no more wit than a cow. And as for being a tempered human being. . . . He always left me with the impression that I was in the presence of nothing more interesting than good old human nature. . . .

I had also met at the Floyd Dells' a man named—well, perhaps he would prefer to remain anonymous. His first name was Dewitt which I didn't at all like. I called him Dick. He was one of those civilized men (to be found exclusively in America it seems) who are more interested in an idea than in a woman. If this isn't quite true at least Dick always made it seem true, which was all that was necessary. It would be difficult for me to express to what

39

point I appreciate this attitude. I may of course be wrong (and of course I don't for a moment think so), but I have always had so little need of the humanity of people. Their humanity is always the same—in bad people (that is, bad-natured because they are always trying to compensate for some lack or hurt) and in good people (those who are on to themselves and who live without fictitious goals). But good or bad they all react in the same way to the great human dramas—love, ambition . . . (are there others?) People's humanity is either bad and boring or good and boring. In both cases one is dragged along the entire gamut of everyday life with them. It is this—the human drama —that has always been unnecessary to me. I don't seem to function in it. At twenty I didn't know as much about it as I do to-day but I knew it wasn't for me. I have always had something to live besides a personal life. And I suspected very early that to live merely in an experience of, in an expression of, in a positive delight in the human clichés could be no business of mine. I have learned nothing from living the humanities. I have learned a great deal from talking about them. With Dick I never had to live a moment of the redundant human exchange. With practically everyone else—men or women—I have had to. I will come to this later—and in case you don't feel it, the tone is grim.

Dick and I talked ideas. Of course we talked monstrously—rather like Oswald Spengler or Evelyn Scott. But this curse can be gradually overcome. By the time I conceived the *Little Review* my conversation had already become more supportable—I spoke only in gasps, gaps and gestures. Dick understood the code and could supply all the words I never had time to stop for. When I hurriedly told him that I was going to publish the best art magazine in the world, he saw the idea perfectly. I was most grateful. People were always telling me that I "saw" their ideas without necessity for formulation on their part. I felt I deserved one friend who could perform this function for me. Dick was the only person who really "saw" the *Little Review*.

He hadn't much money—he was on the staff of an agricultural journal—but he said: You must have that magazine. I can put enough aside each month to pay the printing bill. And office rent. The rest will undoubtedly take care of itself in accordance with those miracles you seem to believe in.

So we dined at the Annex in the white and gold room where Steindhal played Chopin waltzes brilliantly on the piano while reading the newspapers, and we talked of how good the *Little Review* would be. Dick thought it might be just as well to interest certain groups in my project. I didn't. I can't imagine belonging to a group, a Theatre Guild for instance—coöperation, the decision of the majority, the lowest common denominator. . . . I like monarchies, tyrants, prima donnas, the insane. I even like Mussolini—at least *he* is having fun, though Rome is a terrible place to-day.

So I refused any suggestion of group action. I would consent only to the Floyd Dell soirées. At these we discussed names. But no one could think of a good name. I've forgotten what Floyd offered. Arthur Davidson Ficke wanted it called the *March Review* since it was to begin in March. He seemed to feel that this was a charming kind of joke. Finally, in desperation I wanted to call it the *Seagull* (soaring and all that kind of thing). Then I suspected that this was a bit fancy and decided that a simple name like the *Little Review* would be better, the little theatre movement being at the moment in violent vogue. All that group effort resulted in nothing—not even a name.

We decided to honor Clara Laughlin by taking her to tea and telling her all about it. This turned out to be no privilege at all. Clara was more articulate than anyone had yet been about the impossibility of a little review.

Poor innocent, she said, you can't do such a thing. Look at the 'Yellow Book.' It had the backing of John Lane and had everyone on its staff, even Henry James. And it couldn't keep alive a year.

Well, yes, I said, look at the 'Yellow Book.' You can look at it on the library shelves of almost any book lover, richly bound, and rated among his more precious possessions.

Clara continued to discourage us. Fortunately I am never depressed by that kind of argument. If a doctor told me I had a cancer I couldn't manage to believe it with any amount of effort. Somehow I wouldn't feel it to be appropriate. I knew Clara Laughlin was wrong—that she could measure neither my passion, my brain nor my resistance.

Dick may have thought she was right. But it would

have taken a far stronger man to have communicated such a thought to me. Instead he suggested that I go to New York and Boston to get advertisements for the first number. This seemed to me more than good sense.

. . . A train in the late afternoon—the perfect time for departing trains; orchids and chocolates and a book in a lavender cover ("Succession" by Ethel Sidgwick, Small Maynard and Company, Boston). This book I shall never forget—not because of its rather exceptional literary merit but because of its subject matter. It dealt with the impact upon each other of delicate, complex, sensitized, highly organized people—the subject I am always talking about, always defending—the special human being. American life does little to foster the special human being. Other countries do the same. I read "Succession" until the train pulled into New York.

I demanded ads—and got them. I may not be exact but I think I collected four hundred and fifty dollars. Scribner's gave two pages—also Houghton Mifflin. At Appleton's I met Compton McKenzie (good-looking, charming). At Scribner's I met Scott Fitzgerald (also good-looking, charming, smiling, blond, nervous). Scribner's had just moved into their new building in upper Fifth Avenue and Scott Fitzgerald was in Mr. Perkins' office looking over the proofs of his first book, "This Side of Paradise." We talked *Little Review* and I announced what was to be in the first number. Scott regretted with blushes that his stuff was too popular to be solicited by a magazine of the new prose. When I next saw him two years later he was still blushing because he was receiving checks from *Harper's Bazaar,* while good writers like Djuna Barnes had to give their stories to the *Little Review* for nothing.

I don't remember ever having explained to anyone that the *Little Review* couldn't pay for contributions. It was quite taken for granted that since there was no money there would be no talk of remuneration. No one ever asked me why I didn't pay, no one ever urged me to pay, no one ever made me feel that I was robbing the poor artist. It was nine years later in Paris that Gertrude Stein told me I couldn't hope to do such a thing in Europe. Her tone was almost reproachful, although she had always offered her manuscripts to the *Little Review* with the same high disregard of payment that characterized all our contributors. She merely didn't consider it good principle. Well, neither do I consider it good principle for the artist to remain unpaid—it's a little better than for him to remain unprinted, that's all. Practically everything the *Little Review* published during its first years was material that would have been accepted by no other magazine in the world at the moment. Later all the art magazines wanted to print our contributors and, besides, pay them. The contributors took the same stand as Sherwood Anderson. If they had something we especially wanted they gave it to us before the *Dial* was permitted to see it—and pay. The best European writers and painters did the same. I can't help feeling that Gertrude Stein is wrong. I believe that a little review can exist in any country, at any time—not only "before the war." I believe that an analogous thing exists always, somewhere; exists in any epoch of an upheaval in the arts and exists by the same dispensations.

* * * * * *

I came back from New York. We took as an office room 917 in the Fine Arts Building—one of the most delightful buildings in the world I thought, before having seen anything of the world. And still think so, having seen something of it. I went into 917 the moment we signed the lease and spent the first day there alone, staring at the blue walls and living the future of the *Little Review*. I must say I foresaw it accurately—with the possible exception of my criminal record in the United States Courts for publishing the masterpiece of our generation—"Ulysses."

I had written to Galsworthy asking him to send me a word for the first number. It would be difficult for me to remember just why, out of all the world, I chose Galsworthy. I think the emotion of "The Dark Flower" was so close to my own human emotions that I considered its author capable of identifying completely with my art emotions.

We had corrected all the page proofs and were ready

45

for the lock-up when Galsworthy's reply arrived, post-marked Taormina.

My dear Madam:
   You ask me to bid your magazine good speed; and so far as I have any right, I do indeed. It seems you are setting out to watch the street of Life from a high balcony, where at all events the air should be fresh and sunrise sometimes visible. I hope you will decide to sleep out there under the stars, for what kills most literary effort is the hothouse air of temples, clubs, and coteries, that, never changed, breeds in us by turn febrility and torpor. Enthusiasms are more convincing from those who have not told their loves too often. And criticism more poignant from one who has been up at dawn, seen for himself and put down his impression before he goes on 'Change. There is a saying of de Maupassant about a writer sitting down before an object until he has seen it in the way that he alone can see it, seen it with the part of him which makes him This man and not That. For the creative artist and the creative critic there is no rule, I think, so golden. And I did seem to notice in America that there was a good deal of space and not much time; and that without too much danger of becoming "Yogis" people might perhaps sit down a little longer in front of things than they seemed to do. But I noticed too a great energy and hope. These will be your servants to carry through what will not, surely, be just an exploit or adventure, but a true and long comradeship with effort that is worth befriending.
   So all good fortune!

Very faithfully yours,
JOHN GALSWORTHY.

When I read "temple" I was disconcerted. A temple was what I wanted. Not the *petite chapelle* of the æsthetes but a temple of the great, the permanent, versus the transient, the exquisite; the special versus the typical; not the discriminations of the connoisseur but those of the creator; not taste nor the standards of taste, but the perception of the masters. For me there was to be (there always has been) one criterion: the "marked" human being, the consequent "marked" quality of his work. Instead of avoiding all temples because of the risk of finding myself in the wrong one, I knew there was no risk involved—I was in the right one. I hesitated about printing Galsworthy's letter. The career of the *Little Review* as I planned it would be a definite betrayal of his gentle hopes.

The first number betrayed nothing but my adolescence.

Floyd Dell was given an advance copy. He boomed the sale by a long editorial in the *Chicago Evening Post,* reserving his dissension for the last line: Is this new magazine to be given exclusively to praise rather than to the art of criticism?

It contained in fact nothing but praise, and of those phenomena of art and nature that have been most obviously praised since man began. What I needed was not a magazine but a club room where I could have informed disciples twice a week that nature was wonderful, love beautiful, and art inspired. Even the quotations which filled in the short pages were from old sources designed to prove these facts: Poetry is in nature just as much as carbon is.—*Emerson.* Life is like music; it must be composed by ear, feeling and instinct, not by rule.—*Samuel Butler.*

47

It is rhythm that makes music, that makes poetry, that makes pictures; what we are all after is rhythm, and the whole of the young man's life is going to a tune as he walks home, to the same tune as the stars are going over his head. All things are singing together.—*George Moore*. To feel, to do, to stride forward in elation, chanting a poem of triumphant life!—*James Stevens*. I even dragged in Matthew Arnold's most italicized utterance: Culture has one great passion—the passion for sweetness and light. It has one even yet greater!—the passion for making them *prevail*.

I contributed an article about Paderewski and "the artist's eternal striving"; about Galsworthy's "Dark Flower" with "beauty" and "passion" in every second phrase; about William Vaughn Moody's Letters—"unforgettable thing"; about Rupert Brooke's poetry, not only quoting the most obvious lines but explaining them as "rooted deep in the common soil" or "swinging to great heights."

I achieved my own "greatest heights" in an opening editorial: If you've ever read poetry with a feeling that it was your religion, if you've ever come suddenly upon the whiteness of a Venus in a dim, deep room, if, in the early morning, you've watched a bird with great white wings fly straight up into the rose-colored sun. . . . If these things have happened to you and continue to happen until you're left quite speechless with the wonder of it all, then you will understand our hope to bring them nearer to the common experience of the people who read us.

Floyd Dell wrote an article about a lady who said that love was for women one of the most important things in the world, and proving that work and love, and not either of them alone, are the most important things in the world —the supremest expressions of individual life.

Margery Currey and Cornelia Anderson (Sherwood Anderson's first wife) reviewed a book by Ellen Key—a portrait of Rahel Varnhagen, a feminist of a hundred years ago.

Llewellyn Jones wrote an article on the Meaning of Bergsonism. Dr. George Burman Foster began a series of Nietzsche articles—"The Prophet of a New Culture." Eunice Tietjens sent a "Poem to a Lost Friend"—

> Yet, oh, my heart were very fain to-day
> To love you then!

Nicholas Vachel Lindsay offered one of his first poems "How a Little Girl Danced"—

> With foot like the snow
> And step like the rain.

Arthur Davidson Ficke contributed five poems on Japanese prints. George Soule wrote of the "cubist literature" of Gertrude Stein: Her chief characteristics seem to be an aversion to personal pronouns and a strict adherence to simple declarative statements, untroubled by subordinate clauses or phrases of any kind. Her thought,

49

therefore, resolves itself awkwardly in a four-square way. The multiplicity of her planes becomes confusing after a time, but each plane stands alone. . . . But it seems her early work is now getting too obvious and in her 'Portrait of Miss Dodge' she has eliminated verbs and sentence structure entirely, flinging a succession of image-nouns at the reader. One can surely not accuse her of prettiness.

Sherwood Anderson wrote of The New Note:

In the trade of writing the so-called new note is as old as the world. Simply stated, it is a cry for the reinjection of truth and honesty into the craft. . . . In all the world there is no such thing as an old sunrise, an old wind upon the cheeks, or an old kiss from the lips of your beloved; and in the craft of writing there can be no such thing as age in the souls of the young poets and novelists who demand for themselves the right to stand up and be counted among the soldiers of the new. That there are such youths is brother to the fact that there are ardent young cubists and futurists, anarchists, socialists, and feminists; it is the promise of a perpetual sweet new birth of the world; it is as a strong wind come out of the virgin west.

*   *   *   *   *   *

In the excitement of the public's reactions to the first number there was one that distinguished itself. It came in the form of a telephone call.

My name is Charles Zwaska. I think your *Little Review* is wonderful and I want to help you in any way I can. I've broken away from conventional schooling and my time is free. Couldn't I be the office boy or something?

I said yes he could help in a thousand ways. He was seventeen, he joined the staff half an hour after his telephone call, he did all the practical work in the office for years, besides writing occasionally for the magazine, and he always insisted on calling himself the office boy. We called him Cæsar.

*   *   *   *   *   *

In the second number William Butler Yeats addressed American poets:

I have read several times a poem by Nicholas Vachel Lindsay, one which will be in the anthologies, "General Booth enters into Heaven." This poem is stripped bare of ornament; it has an earnest simplicity, a strange beauty, and you know Bacon said, There is no excellent beauty without strangeness.

I have lived a good many years and have read many writers. When I was younger than Mr. Lindsay, and was beginning to write in Ireland, there was all around me the rhetorical poetry of the Irish politicians. We young writers rebelled against that rhetoric. When I went to London I found a group of young lyric writers who were also against rhetoric. We formed the Rhymers' Club. . . . We wanted to get rid not only of rhetoric but of poetic diction. We tried to strip away everything that was artificial, to get a style like speech, as simple as the simplest prose, like a cry of the heart. . . .

And now there is a group of younger poets who dare to call us rhetorical. When I returned to London from Ireland, I had a young man go over all my work with me to eliminate the abstract. This was an American poet, Ezra Pound.

51

Sherwood Anderson wrote more about The New Note:

> What I quarrel with is writers who look outside themselves for their material. Even realists have done this—as, for example, Howells; and to that extent have failed. The master Zola failed here. Why do we so prize the work of Whitman, Tolstoy, Dostoievsky, Twain, and Fielding? Is it not because as we read we are constantly saying to ourselves, "This book is true"? . . . In this connection I am tempted to give you the substance of a formula I have just worked out. It lies here before me, and if you will accept it in the comradely spirit in which it is offered I shall be glad. It is the most delicate and the most unbelievably difficult task to catch, understand, and record your own mood . . . The practice of constantly and persistently making such a record as this will prove invaluable to the person who wishes to become a true critic of writing in the new spirit.

As for my own contributions I toned down somewhat my desperate ardor for art, influenced not only by the letters of criticism that poured in (all of which I printed in the second number) but also by those of too-sentimental congratulation. This attitude brought forth a protest, in the third number, from a disappointed Russian, Alexander Kaun, who missed the sea-gull and the morning sun:

> The crime of the April number lies in the fact of its closely following (chronologically) the issue of March. In the beginning you appeared to us as a prophet . . . now you have degenerated into a priest. Don't you think there are already more priests than worshippers in our Temple? . . . Your debut was

a revelation, a new word . . . it was a wonderful number, all fresh and beautiful. Now you have turned your temple into a parliament of dissonances; you have admitted Victorian ladies and sentimental crucifiers of Nietzsche. Then that cacophony of personal letters: I blushed at the sight of these tokens of familiarity and tappings over your shoulder on the part of the benevolent readers. I wished to shout to the Misses Jones to keep off the altar, lest they besmirch your white robe with their penny compliments and saccharine effusions . . . I read with delight your quotation of Wilde's paradox: "There is nothing sane about the worship of beauty. It is entirely too splendid to be sane." I fear you are getting too sane—you who in my illusion I pictured enthroned in a tower, high above the street and the crowd, perceiving reality through dim stained glass walls. Alas, there is evidently an accommodating lift that connects your tower with the side-walk. You have become so sane, so logical, so militant in attacking the obvious. . . . Oh, Pan and Apollo!

* * * * * *

Rupert Brooke appeared upon the horizon of America, and the world of Chicago turned out to pay him tribute. Yeats had written that he had the beauty of a god (I quote inexactly) and wore the handsomest cravats in London. The first statement could be taken literally. The second had no relation to the reality. Rupert Brooke dressed spotlessly, though as carelessly as any poet I have ever known—always excluding Max Bodenheim. He gave the impression in fact of wearing the hob-nailed boots ascribed to him by a Boston editorial.

Maurice Browne of the Chicago Little Theatre brought

him to the *Little Review* studio. He was as shy as a girl—an English girl. His beauty was a girl's beauty. When he walked on Michigan Boulevard everyone turned to watch him—not because he was always recognized as Rupert Brooke, but because of the fairness of his look. Had he left off his slightly too large black hat and shown his hair he would have rivaled Bernhardt as publicity material. He walked with the stride of the Cambridge man but without the Cambridge arrogance. His stride was long and loose, but he was intent.

We lunched and he promised some poems for the *Little Review*. I wanted something of the Helen quality ("her head bent down in such a way") and he laughed and said he would try. He was to be in Chicago only a few days and then to go on to the west. His American publishers had asked Arthur Davidson Ficke to do a biographical sketch of him and Ficke was eager to begin.

I shall dog your footsteps, he said to the poet, now that I'm to be your official biographer.

Rupert Brooke laughed too, but remotely. It's an awkward relationship, he said.

*　　*　　*　　*　　*　　*

May . . . and the third number of the *Little Review* was going to press. I heard Emma Goldman lecture and had just time to turn anarchist before the presses closed.

I wrote an article beginning with a passionate question as to why anyone wanted to own property, why people didn't live as brothers, and why didn't they understand

MARGARET ANDERSON

MARGARET ANDERSON

Photograph by Victor Georg

jh

Photograph by E. O. Hoppé

EDITORS OF THE LITTLE REVIEW

a page from the Little Review, Vol. IX, No. 2

JANE HEAP
photograph by Berenice Abbott

The beach at Braeside

"CAESAR" ZWASKA

HARRIET DEAN

THE LITTLE REVIEW

THE WILD STAR
by Witter Bynner

There is a star whose bite is certain death
While the moon but makes you mad—
So run from stars till you are out of breath
On a spring-night, my lad,
Or slip among the shadows of a pine
And hide face down from the sky
And never stir and never make a sign
Till the wild star goes by.

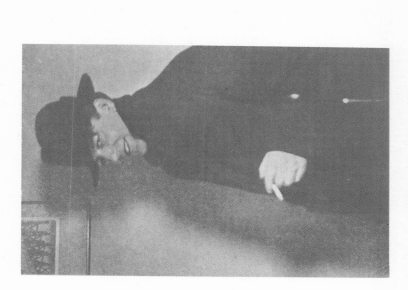

RICHARD ALDINGTON

BEN HECHT
photograph by M. Goldberg

Jane's portrait
of Amy Lowell.

Exact likeness.

Margaret Anderson's comment on a caricature by Jane Heap

GATHERING HER OWN FIRE-WOOD

SWIMMING

THE STEED ON WHICH SHE HAS
HER PICTURE TAKEN

THE INSECT ON WHICH SHE RIDES

"Light occupations of the editor [Margaret Anderson] while
there is nothing to edit." Center spread drawn by Jane Heap
for the "blank issue" of the Little Review, Vol. XII, No. 2

HAROLD BAUER

Yes, I received your circular, and now receive its duplicate with your letter.

This is what happened. I spoke to my Psyche about the questionnaire, very cautiously, for she is quite an old fashioned female and has prejudices against peek-a-bo garments. She immediately burst into tears, saying : "so THIS is what you think of me !" and threatened to go home to mother if I ever referred to the subject again.

Put yourselves in my place, M. A. and J. H. She may be an ill-favored virgin, but she is mine own and no one else's. I can't afford to lose her, as I am too old to get another mistress.

All cordial greetings from

HAROLD BAUER

MARY GARDEN
a page from the Little Review, Vol. III, No. 9

ALEXANDER BERKMAN
photograph by Berenice Abbott

EMMA GOLDMAN
photograph by Berenice Abbott

"THE BARONESS"
a page from the Little Review, Vol. VII, No. 3

THE LITTLE REVIEW

Art and the Law

by jh

THE heavy farce and sad futility of trying a creative work in a court of law appalls me. Was there ever a judge qualified to judge even the simplest psychic outburst? How then a work of Art? Has any man not a nincompoop ever been heard by a jury of his peers?

In a physical world laws have been made to preserve physical order. Laws cannot reach, nor have power over, any other realm. Art is and always has been the supreme Order. Because of this it is the only activity of man that has an eternal quality. Works of Art are the only permanent sign that man has existed. What legal genius to bring Law against Order!

The society for which Mr. Sumner is agent, I am told, was founded to protect the public from corruption. When asked *what public?* its defenders spring to the rock on which America was founded: the cream-puff of sentimentality, and answer chivalrously "Our young girls." So the mind of the young girl rules this country? In it rests the safety, progress and lustre of a nation. One might have guessed it. . . . but—why is she given such representatives? I recall a photograph of the United States Senators, a galaxy

The beginning of an editorial by Jane Heap on the
"Ulysses Trial", from the Little Review, Vol. VII, No. 3

DJUNA BARNES
photograph by Berenice Abbott

EZRA POUND
photograph by Man Ray

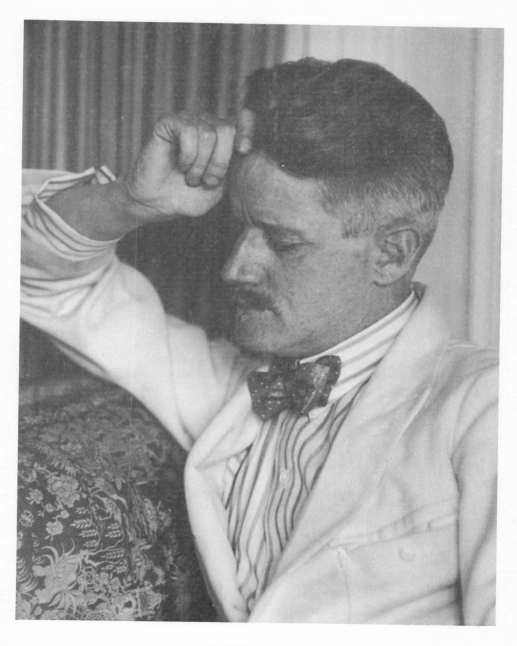

JAMES JOYCE
photographs by Berenice Abbott

THE LITTLE REVIEW

Vol. V.   MARCH, 1918   No. 11

ULYSSES

JAMES JOYCE

Episode 1

STATELY, plump Buck Mulligan came from the stairhead, bearing a bowl of lather on which a mirror and a razor lay crossed. A yellow dressing gown, ungirdled, was sustained gently behind him on the mild morning air. He held the bowl aloft and intoned:

—*Introibo ad altare Dei.*

Halted, he peered down the dark winding stairs and called up coarsely:

—Come up, Kinch. Come up, you fearful jesuit.

Solemnly he came forward and mounted the round gunrest. He faced about and blessed gravely thrice the tower, the surrounding country and the awaking mountains. Then, catching sight of Stephen Dedalus, he bent towards him and made rapid crosses in the air, gurgling in his throat and shaking his head. Stephen Dedalus, displeased and sleepy, leaned his arms on the top of the staircase and looked coldly at the shaking gurgling face that blessed him, equine in its length, and at the light untonsured hair, grained and hued like pale oak.

Buck Mulligan peeped an instant under the mirror and then covered the bowl smartly.

—Back to barracks, he said sternly.

He added in a preacher's tone:

—For this, O dearly beloved, is the genuine christine: body and soul and blood and ouns. Slow music, please. Shut your eyes, gents. One moment. A little trouble about those white corpuscles. Silence, all.

The beginning of the Ulysses serialization

he should arrive at Phibsborough more quickly by a triple change of tram or by hailing a car or on foot through Smithfield, ~~Grangegorman~~ Constitution hill and Broadstone ~~terminus~~.

242

William Humble, earl of Dudley, and Lady Dudley, accompanied by lieutenantcolonel Hesseltine, drove out after luncheon from the viceregal lodge. In the following carriage were the honourable Mrs Paget, Miss de Courcy and the honourable Gerald Ward A. D. C. in attendance.

The cavalcade passed out by the lower gate of Phœnix Park saluted by obsequious policemen and proceeded along the northern quays. The viceroy was most cordially greated on his way through the metropolis. At Bloody bridge Mr Thomas Kernan beyond the river greeted him vainly from afar. In the porch of Four Courts Richie Goulding with the costsbag of Goulding, Collis and Ward saw him with surprise. At the doorstep of the office of Reuben J. Dodd, solicitor, agent for the Patriotic Insurance Company, an elderly female about to enter changed her plan and retracing her steps by King's windows smiled credulously on the representative of His Majesty. From its sluice in Wood quay wall under Tom Devan's office Poddle river hung out in fealty a tongue of liquid sewage. Above the crossblind of the Ormond Hotel, bronze by gold, Miss Kennedy's head by Miss Douce's head watched and admired. On Ormond quay Mr Simon Dedalus, steering his way from the greenhouse for the subsheriff's office, stood still in midstreet and brought his hat low. His Excellency graciously returned Mr Dedalus greeting. From Cahill's corner the reverend Hugh C. Love made obeisance unperceived, mindful of lords deputies whose hands benignant had held of yore rich advowsons. On Grattan bridge Lenehan and M'Coy, taking leave of each other, watched the carriages go by. Passing by Roger Greene's office and Dollard's big red printinghouse Gerty Mac Dowell, carrying the Catesby's cork lino letters for her father who was laid up, knew by the style it was the lord and lady lieutenant but she couldn't see what her Excellency had on because the tram and Spring's big yellow furniture van had to stop in front of her on account of its being the lord lieutenant. From the shaded door of Kavanagh's winerooms John Wyse Nolan smiled with unseen coldness towards the lord lieutenantgeneral and general governor of Ireland. Over against Dame gate Tom Rochford and Nosey Flynn watched the approach of the cavalcade. Tom Rochford, seeing the eyes of lady Dudley fixed on him, took his thumbs quickly out of the pockets of his claret waistcoat and doffed his cap to her. A charming *soubrette*, great Marie Kendall, with dauby cheeks and lifted skirt, smiled daubily from her poster

1. Between Queen's and Whitworth bridges (the) viceregal carriages passed and were unsaluted by Mr Dudley White, B.L., M.A., who stood on Arran Quay outside Mrs M.E. White's, the pawnbroker's, at the corner of Arran street west stroking his nose with his forefinger, undecided whether

F past Kingsbridge

7o X

2. Past Richmond bridge at (separate)

V, M.A.,

= H

1= Lord Dudley's

X

A

C

#

V.

Joyce kept adding to Ulysses after it appeared in the Little Review, as this page of first edition proof shows. (Courtesy of Lockwood Memorial Library, State University of New York at Buffalo)

GEORGE ANTHEIL
at Bernardsville

MARGARET ANDERSON *and* ALLEN TANNER
in the basement at Bernardsville

Rear view of the house at Brookhaven

GEORGETTE LEBLANC and ALLEN TANNER
at Brookhaven

WYNDHAM LEWIS

Recent photograph

a photograph from the final number of the Little Review, Vol. XII, No. 2

GERTRUDE STEIN
photograph by Man Ray

ERNEST HEMINGWAY

Photograph : Helen Breaker

42

VALENTINE

For a Mr. Lee Wilson Dodd and Any of His Friends
who Want it.

Sing a song of critics
pockets full of lye
four and twenty critics
hope that you will die
hope that you will peter out
hope that you will fail
so they can be the first one
be the first to hail
any happy weakening or sign of quick decay.
(All are very much alike, weariness too great,
sordid small catastrophies, stack the cards on fate,
very vulgar people, annals of the callous,
dope fiends, soldiers, prostitutes,
men without a gallus*)
If you do not like them lads
one thing you can do
stick them up your. . . . . lads
My Valentine to you.

ERNEST HEMINGWAY

a page from the final number of the Little Review, Vol. XII, No. 2

PABLO PICASSO
photograph by Man Ray

CONSTANTIN BRANCUSI
photograph by Man Ray

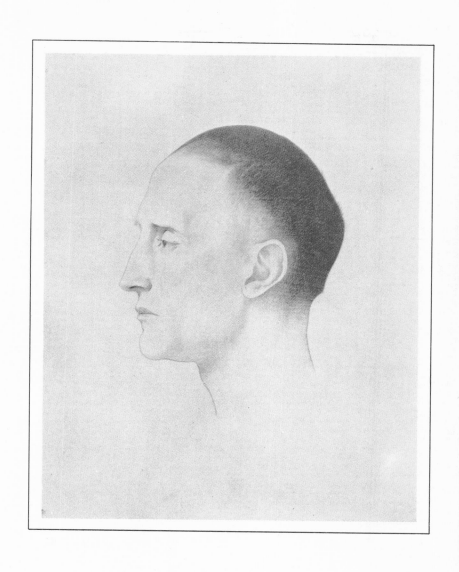

MARCEL DUCHAMP
a drawing by Joseph Stella from the Little Review, Vol. IX, No. 1

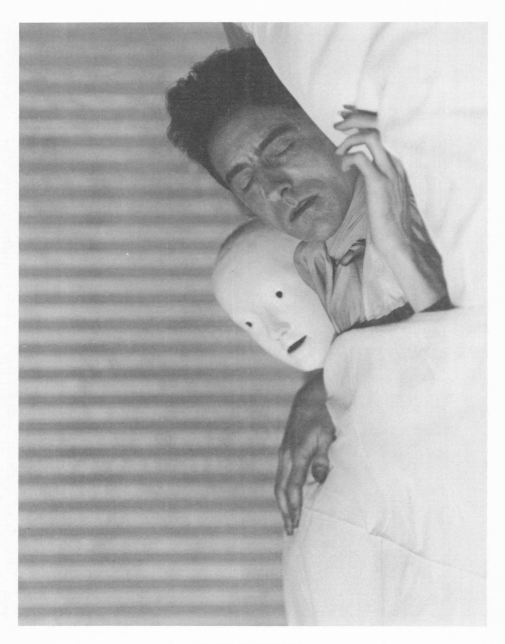

JEAN COCTEAU
photograph by Berenice Abbott

GEORGE ANTHEIL
photograph by Berenice Abbott

GEORGETTE LEBLANC
drawing by Djuna Barnes

the anarchist religion. I lauded Emma Goldman. Her name was enough in those days to produce a shudder. She was considered a monster, an exponent of free love and bombs. Her lecture was my first contact with the astounding truth that popular legend is usually in direct contradiction to the facts. It seemed to me that any average intelligence should have been equal to the feat of seeing Emma Goldman as she was: a whole-hearted idealist—oh, very ideal—with humanity as her personal problem. She hadn't an idea that any decent person doesn't start life with—and end it with for that matter. An idea? I should say an emotion—an elementary emotion about the vileness of human behavior. Well, she should know rather better than most of us how vile it is. She was put in prison for nothing at all—for being thoroughly nice, you might say, if you were pushed for a reason—and banished from her chosen land for some as yet undefined incompatibility between herself and the government.

My stimulating remarks about her first lecture were not propitious for my personal destiny. After the May number had circulated with surprising but satisfying scandal, Dick came to see me one day. It was a rainy day. I remember because he wore a rain coat in which he didn't look his best. He should have looked his best because he had come in distress and on difficult business. He had made a decision. He presented it with such embarrassment and hesitation that I felt it my duty to guess what he wanted to say and say it for him—which is fairly often my lot in life. He had decided he could no longer continue his association with a magazine that was going anarchist . . . he would lose his position . . . would find himself without funds for the *Little Review* . . . and so it would be better. . . .

I knew that he knew the fanaticism with which I would have proclaimed him incapable of such an act. So I imagined that he was feeling worse than I was. My only impulse was to relieve him of his pain and to spare him any repercussions of what might have become a first-rate human drama. . . . Considering the realities involved, our interview should have been momentous. But from the moment I divined what he wanted to say (which was immediately) it didn't last ten minutes. My brain worked with its customary and comforting rapidity: rather serious, what can I do? . . . any number of things . . . chiefly not worry poor Dick who appears to be dying as it is . . . nothing can stop the *Little Review* . . . I'm equal to any emergency . . . produce a few more miracles. . . .

Within ten minutes I had managed to convey all this to him and suggested that we talk of something else. Dick returned to life and we had a charming intellectual conversation.

But worse was to come. I had word that the family was moving to Chicago.

I had last visited them in a house like a country club in Springfield, Illinois, and had every reason to hope that its unique attraction would retain them for longer than the usual year. If they came to Chicago my life would be devastated again. Mother would try to stop the *Little Review*. There would be weary hours of invective against Richard Aldington for praising a woman's breast in a poem. It would be assumed that I would live at home, everyone agreeing to be polite, and then one evening mother would decide to have it out with me about the relative merits of Christian Science and anarchism. I would seriously waste hours contrasting the unchallengable loftiness of anarchism with the virtues of Christian Science. I would urge her to remain a Christian Scientist if she would allow me to remain an anarchist. This would be considered illogical. Mother would spend the rest of the night denying the existence of evil but finding me very evil. . . .

These home pictures were driving me mad when I was suddenly tempted, through an irresistible appeal to my lower nature, to risk them: an apartment on the lake, "on" meaning three feet from the water's edge—the north side, Ainslee Street. The lake filled every window. For me there was a room and bath like a dream of spring—pale green walls, wistaria hangings, a pink rug, a large yellow lamp, a blue lake. . . . It was widely separated from the rest of the apartment. If one locked door didn't insulate me I could entrench myself behind two, in the bathroom. I could spend my home life bathing.

I spent the first night in the bathroom reading Blake.

I was having a marvelous time being an editor. I was born to be an editor. I always edit everything. I edit my room at least once a week. Hotels are made for me. I can change a hotel room so thoroughly that even its proprietor doesn't recognize it. I select or reject every house seen from train windows and install myself in all the chosen ones, changing their defects, of course. Life becomes confusing. . . . Where haven't I lived?

I edit people's clothes, dressing them infallibly in the right lines. I am capable of becoming so obsessed by the lines of a well-cut coat that its owner thinks I am flirting with him before I've realized he is in the coat. I change everyone's coiffure—except those that please me—and these I gaze at with such satisfaction that I become suspect. I edit people's tones of voice, their laughter, their words. I change their gestures, their photographs. I change the books I read, the music I hear. In a passing glance I know a man's sartorial perfections or crimes—collar, cravat, handkerchief, socks, cut of shoulders, lapels, trousers, placement of waistline, buttons, pockets, quality of material, shoes, walk, manner of carrying stick, angle of hat, contour of hair. It is this incessant, unavoidable observation, this need to distinguish and impose, that has made me an editor. I can't make things. I can only revise what has been made. And it is this eternal revising that has given me my nervous face.

I now had no living expenses and could pour that economy into the *Little Review*. Two days a week I held my nerves in control and edited a book page for the *Continent*. This meant forty dollars a month—enough for the studio rent and a savings account of five dollars. The savings went for concerts.

Someone sent in a poem with a line I still remember without references to the back files (which I haven't anyway)—"moon paint on a colorless house." I sent for the poet who turned out to be Maxwell Bodenheim. He smoked a long white malodorous pipe. Sometimes he decorated it with a large knot of baby blue ribbon—toward what end I have never discovered. His eyes were the same blue. It may have been that.

Everybody came to the studio. Ben Hecht with his "pale green face," his genius for adjectives, his tender cynicism for my enthusiasms.

You stole my metaphor. I was just going to compare the piano to the Winged Victory myself. It's a shame, because you can't write. I'll teach you to write if you like.

I don't like. I'm not a writer. I will never be one. I'm merely an inspiration to writers—I tell them what they should be. Ben Hecht for instance should be a decadent rather than a socialist.

Carl Sandburg was intensely socialist and was publishing a working-man's daily. Then he suddenly began to write poems and chants which he intoned in such a deep voice that the studio furniture shook under its vibrations. He lived a domestic suburban life but tramped the Chicago streets composing his working-man's saga.

Edgar Lee Masters was the funny man of the *literati*.

His eyes twinkled (it's the only verb) and he indulged with obvious pleasure in the lowest slap-stick humor. He looked like Thackeray. His "Spoon River Anthology" had just been published in *Poetry*, Harriet Monroe's magazine of verse which bore the ill-advised slogan of Whitman's: "To have great poets we must have great audiences too." Not true, however you look at it. Great poets create great audiences, just as great people create their experiences instead of being created by them.

* * * * * *

Harriet Monroe appeared at the door of 917 one morning with a visitor—a large and important visitor whom I have always considered among the most charming people I have known. Physically she was of such vastness that she entered the door with difficulty. She came from Brookline, Massachusetts, and her name was Amy Lowell. On my last trip to New York she had telephoned me from Brookline and I had visualized her, from her high rapid telephone voice, as a slender and imperious blond. She had wanted me to rush to Brookline and tell her about the *Little Review*. But I hadn't gone, being pressed for time. We had corresponded since that time and she had sent me poems for the magazine.

She was dressed that morning in the mode of *Godey's Lady's Book*. Culture and good taste were stamped upon her. She was brunette, her voice was contralto, her nose like a Roman emperor's and her manner somewhat more masterful. But I learned later she wept on the slightest

60

provocation and had more feminine whims and humors than any ten women.

Her first words were congenial to me.

I've had a fight with Ezra Pound. When I was in London last fall (spring, summer?) I offered to join his group and put the Imagists on the map. Ezra refused. All right, my dear chap, I said, we'll see who's who in this business. I'll go back to America and advertise myself so extensively that you'll wish you had come in with me.

I gathered that she wanted to subsidize modern poetry and push it ahead faster than it could go by its own impetus. A little review would be a helpful organ for such a purpose.

I love the *Little Review*, she went on, and I have money. You haven't. Take me in with you. I'll pay you one hundred and fifty dollars a month, you'll remain in full control, I'll merely direct your poetry department. You can count on me never to dictate.

No clairvoyance was needed to know that Amy Lowell would dictate, uniquely and majestically, any adventure in which she had a part. I should have preferred being in the clutches of a dozen groups. So I didn't hesitate. I was barely polite.

It's charming of you but I couldn't think of it.

Your reasons?

I have only one. I can't function in 'association.'

Amy was furious. She concealed it. She argued, implored. I could see that she had set her mind on the idea. But she had a redeeming trait—when she was finally con-

61

vinced that I meant what I said she dropped the subject
and never reverted to it.

Come and lunch with me to-morrow at the Annex. . . .

When I went in she was sitting in a huge armchair, enveloped in a huge lounging robe, smoking a huge cigar.

Have a cigarette. *I* smoke cigars.

She had taken a suite, brought a friend, a secretary and
a staff of servants with her. Her meals were served in her
apartment. She was sensitive about her size and never
appeared in public. After lunch she dressed in her severe
clothes and hat and told a servant to call a taxi.

Come with me. I'm going to Eugene Hutchinson in
the Fine Arts Building to have my picture taken.

You won't need a taxi, I said. The Fine Arts Building is next door.

I always ride.

And so we stepped into the taxi . . . and stepped out
again.

Amy Lowell couldn't have liked to write letters. Her
conversation was often prose of quality, but the prose of
her letters was oftener that of a business man.

* * * * * *

The summer passed. September came. And with it my
first knowledge of tragedy and death.

One night mother and dad were playing bridge in the
apartment across the hall. I was playing the piano. The

door bell rang sharply and repeatedly. I rushed to open. Mother stood there, terror in her eyes. Her voice, hands and face were shaking.

Something has happened to your father. He suddenly threw his cards on the table and began to laugh foolishly and say words that had no sense.

That had continued for a full minute. Then he picked up his cards and began to talk quite naturally. But he watched the others with piteous eyes, as if he were asking himself if anything had happened. They all pretended that nothing had.

A certitude flashed upon me. Nothing had prepared us. Except—now that we had to seek causes—several things. He had been coming home from business at four o'clock and sleeping with voracity until six or seven. This was unheard of. He had talked of escaping the pressure of work in his offices by taking daily motor trips. Also I remembered his telling me in the spring of a curious sensation in the back of his head—a whirring and upward rush like the spraying of a fountain. He had spoken of it as of an interesting, untroubling phenomenon. Even more significant—in January he had decided to take a pleasure trip to Florida. He had never in his life planned a pleasure for himself alone. He would have wanted us all to go to Florida. I remember his announcing, as though it were a treachery which gave him an unpardonable but strange delight, that he thought he would enjoy seeing Florida. So he had gone.

September first had been his fiftieth birthday. He had

63

always had a fear of being fifty. It had seemed age to him and a confession of failure—life lived for nothing, not even for the accumulation of money, since money doesn't accumulate when it is squandered. What would become of us? Four extravagant women. A life of life insurance?

We went on pretending that nothing had happened; but had great doctors—specialists who demanded blood tests and found a blood singularly pure; alienists who talked of the great American tragedy—repression. And the symptoms increased daily: twenty-dollar tips to taxi-drivers for trips amounting to a dollar and a half; a furtive manner of devouring food; innocent obscenities, since no obscene word had ever passed his lips. There were no delusions of grandeur. There was only the obsession of happiness.

I am finding a better position for the cook's husband. From now on he will have a salary of a million a year. That will make them quite comfortable and happy.

He noted the addresses of the laundress, the butcher boy, the ice-man, the grocer. They were all to have several hundred thousand dollars annually. His face as he talked of these arrangements was terribly happy. All his friends were provided with millions. And for him there was no provision—since there is none. Sanitariums and ten months later—death.

*　　*　　*　　*　　*　　*

Late in the following July mother and I reached our breaking point.

Her ultimatum was that I must not live my life, think my thoughts, publish my magazine. I must live her life as dad had done.

Dick had given Jean a little dog. He was sad discreet and infinitesimal, but it was upon him that the situation turned. Mother came home and saw him; and incidentally saw Jean's radiant face. She said she wouldn't have a dog in the house. I couldn't quite stand Jean's crying, so I began to argue.

We talked until five o'clock in the morning. Christian Science came in for at least four hours. The rest of the time I analyzed the causes of dad's breakdown and explained that I could not consciously allow the same forces to overtake me; that we must decide finally which policy was to rule our house—hers of suppression or mine of freedom.

No one has ever talked like this to her mother.

It is life or death for me—it must be decided.

I will break you. I will leave Chicago within three days and go home to live. I will take all the furniture in the apartment.

That is a good idea. Your friends are there. You'll be happier.

You can't live without furniture.

Oh, yes, I can very well live without furniture.

You have nothing, since all the money is in my name. You can't pay a hundred dollars a month for this apartment.

I will think of something.

We shall see.

We saw the next morning—saw the moving men come in to make an estimate on the packing.

I explained to Jean. I have made a decision. Do you want to go or stay with me?

Stay of course.

Starting downtown, I met mother at the door. She was surprisingly nice to me—nicer than she had ever been. She looked happier and I felt relieved.

The packing of the furniture went on. Jean spent the days with me in the Fine Arts Building, helping with the crisis of going to press. Three or four days later we went home one night, leaving the *Little Review* ready for distribution.

The apartment was marvelous . . . nude as the day it was built. Nothing but the lake and the stars in the windows; not a chair, rug, book or clock . . . Finally in one of the bedrooms two objects timidly emerged—two small beds that belonged to me. And on the window ledge in the kitchen were two knives, two forks, two spoons. Jean wasn't daunted and I was lyrical.

This is the way it should be. One should begin life all over again every few years. Now we can start clear. It's *my* life and those that like it can share it. It will be beautiful.

We moved the beds into separate windows. The lake was soft and quiet. The stars were falling. I counted six and waited a long while for the seventh. Then I closed my eyes. I wanted only seven.

The next morning I had a pressing thing to do. I went to the Mason and Hamlin Piano Company on Wabash Avenue and asked for Mr. Ryder.

A few months before I had written an article contrasting the playing of Paderewski with that of Harold Bauer. In the article, without any thought of advertising, I had compared the Mason Hamlin and the Steinway pianos. The two pianists had given concerts on the same day. I had gone to the first half of Bauer's and then rushed to Paderewski's—torn by such a conflict as I rarely have to face. (I can never leave anything before the end, and I always arrive for the beginning.) The Steinway had sounded inadequate after listening to the Mason Hamlin. So I had put this crude fact into writing with an unassailable naïveté. And now that our apartment was pianoless I saw a way of putting the article to use.

Mr. Ryder had read the article and had "found it very true." Of course. I deserved a small Mason and Hamlin grand. If I would give them a yearly ad in the *Little Review* free of charge he would rent me a piano free of charge. I chose the piano from among a hundred, giving the day to it. Jean and I waited at home the next morning for its arrival. We spent the afternoon pacing the empty apartment in order to burst suddenly into the living room and be startled by it standing there against the windows and the lake.

Jean was invited to visit friends and Harriet Dean of

Indianapolis asked if she could fill the vacant post on the *Little Review*. Harriet was worshipful about the L.R. (She worshiped for two years, denying herself all possible comforts to keep it alive, turning anarchist, since that was the fashion, and hurling at everyone quotations from what I had said on page so and so. Then one day she didn't know what it had all been about—either her enthusiasm or the L.R. She became an intellectual, they tell me.)

The present staff comprised Cæsar and Harriet Dean. We inaugurated subscription campaigns to pay for the apartment and the printing, ate when we could, and Harriet moved into the vacant apartment and the vacant bed. There were always the two bathrooms and the shower which, being attached, couldn't leave for another city. So we were very clean. We bought towels at the ten-cent store and a few cushions for the sun porch. Furniture was undesirable, I decided—encumbrant. There was the piano stool. . . .

Eunice Tietjens came out, bringing a diamond ring.

I don't want this any more. Sell it and bring out an issue.

Everyone helped. People stopped me in the street.

Aren't you Margaret Anderson? Congratulations!

Chicago was thrilling. Such smiling excitement, such a confederacy of protection around us as the inspired youth of the age.

You can't be as valiant as you look, someone told me.

You look like the prow of a ship advancing in the street, said someone else.

This flattery encouraged me to walk as rhythmically

as possible. I walked to music—usually a Kreisler waltz—as I found by experimenting that three-four time produced a more billowy movement than two-four. Bert Leston Taylor, one of the first of the columnists (*Chicago Tribune*) named me Colonel Anderson and related my Nietzschean exploits. Frank Lloyd Wright gave me a hundred dollars when I began raising funds to keep alive.

Never be ashamed to ask help for good work, he admonished me, seeing that I disliked the rôle of money-raising.

Unknown people asked me to lunch, urged me to talk about my "ideals," and the next day sent a hundred dollars for the ideals. Even the waiter at Pittsburg Joe's (where we ate when funds were low) talked Max Stirner with me.

My attitude during this epoch was: Life is just one ecstasy after another.

* * * * * *

Emma Goldman had written how much she appreciated my article on anarchism. Now she wrote again that she was passing through Chicago and would like to see me.

I was exalted. To know the great martyred leader! I thought the lake and the empty apartment would be soothing to her so I asked her to stay with us while she was in Chicago.

She answered, thanking me graciously, but explaining that she never visited families, that she couldn't adapt herself to bourgeois life even for a few days. I replied that we weren't exactly bourgeois perhaps—that we ought to be very congenial to her, being without furniture. But she didn't believe it, I think. She wanted to see.

She asked me to come to the Lexington Hotel to talk with her, which I quickly did. As my elevator reached her floor she was standing near it, waiting for me. She wore a flowered summer dress and a straw hat with a ribbon. She was made all of one piece. When I stepped from the elevator she turned her back on me. I was amazed and hurt. I decided that I probably looked so frivolous she was scorning me. But I took courage and asked her if she weren't Miss Goldman, and she turned a welcoming face to me, saying she had been sure it wasn't I. Later she explained that this was because I looked too chic. She hadn't been prepared for it.

She had some people in her room—the fantastic Dr. Ben Reitman (who wasn't so bad if you could hastily drop all your ideas as to how human beings should look and act) and a beautiful woman with white hair who resembled a czarina. She had an ailing heart and made me think of Yeats' poem to Aubrey Beardsley's sister. She was flamingly revolted by everything and, though she had been born in a conventional world, had lived her life highly and thought anarchists and I.W.W.'s a little tame. She was never precise about what should be done to the offending bourgeois but it was always something unthinkably scathing. We became great friends.

Emma Goldman surprised me by being more human

than she had seemed on the platform. When she lectured she was as serious as the deep Russian soul itself. In private she was gay, communicative, tender. Her English was the peculiar personal idiom favored by Russian Jews and she spoke only in platitudes—which I found fascinating. Her eyes were a clear strong blue which deepened as she talked.

She asked me to lunch the next day and we went into the Auditorium Hotel. It was Sunday and there were few people. I wanted stories of her life and loved her way of telling them. I asked for the McKinley story. So she told me of the fair-haired blue-eyed boy she had met one day in a library in Cleveland. She had been startled when he presented himself, looking like an angel and explaining that he had read her philosophy of anarchism. She never saw him again, never heard from him, never heard of him again until "the country was ringing" with the assassination. She was almost mobbed and narrowly escaped being held responsible for the crime. I asked her how she explained such acts.

Who knows the human soul? she asked slowly.

I couldn't continue calling her Miss Goldman and her request to be called Emma was beyond me. I don't believe I could call any human being Emma. I suggested naming her "E.G.," which pleased her. She was by this time entirely reassured as to my unbourgeois nature, and eager to see the empty apartment.

I went to the Lexington to fetch her and her bag (it deserves mention, being so big) and as we stood at the door of the hotel waiting for a trolley car a proletarian chose that moment to fall off a truck he was driving. He slid down from his high seat and floundered among the horses' feet with horrible noises. E.G.'s coördination was something to remark—her cry and act were simultaneous. She pulled the man from under the horses before anyone else on the street could move and administered first aid with such a grim face that I felt she might be planning to hit him on the jaw as soon as she had revived him. But I learned later that she was always grim when distressed. I have seen beggars in the street ask her for money and my instinct was always to conceal myself under the sidewalk until the bout was over—she looked as if she would knock out the universe.

The truckman wasn't ruined and we went on to the North Side. E.G. was grim all the way. She relaxed when she saw the apartment and saw that I hadn't exaggerated about the furniture. I urged her to have a chair (piano stool) and not to worry about capitalism while she was with us. She laughed and said she saw none to worry about.

Harriet Dean came in to meet her. Harriet had such an emphatic handshake, such a Rooseveltian smile, and was in such haste to assure E.G. of her impulse to knock the blocks off tyrants and oppressors that E.G. adopted her at once. We dined lightly (on superlative coffee made by E.G.) and then walked on the beach as the night came down. No one else was there. E.G. sang Russian folk songs in a low and husky voice. We were immensely moved.

And then the great anarchist could control her enthusiasm no longer. She telephoned to Reitman and a few "comrades" to come out.

It's divine here, she cried.

They came and also found it divine.

You look rejuvenated, Emma, they exclaimed, rushing through the apartment with violence. I was glad there was no furniture. . . .

Bill Haywood was with them but as always gave the impression of being alone. He didn't inspect the apartment. He sat powerfully on a window ledge and talked of small dogs.

Can you stand seeing rich women with lapdogs? he asked. I can't. When I think of the thousands of children who are in want—and then those women with their dogs —well, it makes me sick.

This was almost his only remark. Someone recited Whitman's "Come lovely and smiling death," and he bowed his head in approval. He had only one eye and at that moment it was full of tears.

Play for us, E.G. demanded. And I, feeling unselfconscious for the first time in my life, played the piano for an hour. They all sat silent.

You're a great artist, said E.G. authoritatively.

It was the first time in my magazine-cover existence

73

that I had been taken at another valuation. I was filled with gratitude.

Two days later the agent of our building came to see me with a determined face.

We've had complaints that Emma Goldman has been here. We can't allow such a thing.

I was charmed to enlighten him. I made him sit on the piano stool. I produced pamphlets on anarchism. I read passages. I explained the difference between philosophical and bomb-throwing anarchism. I stated that it was an honor to have Emma Goldman in the house as contrasted with the bridge-playing protoplasms that infested the rest of the building. I was working up to my climax when he seemed to get bored. He left and never came back.

I became increasingly anarchistic. I began to find people of my own class vicious, people in clean collars uninteresting. I even accepted smells, personal as well as official. Everyone who came to the studio smelled either of machine oil or herring.

Anarchism was the ideal expression for my ideas of freedom and justice. The knowledge that people could be put into prisons and kept there for life had the power to torture me. That human beings could be sentenced to death by other human beings was a fact beyond human imagination. I decided that I would make my life a crusade against inhumanity.

74

One day the papers announced that the governor of Utah had refused to pardon an anarchist condemned to death for—I've forgotten what—nothing at all as I remember, like Sacco and Vanzetti. I wrote an editorial ending with the cry: Why doesn't someone shoot the governor of Utah?

Detectives came to the studio. I happened not to be there (to my regret). A man from New York—an influential person I had met at dinner the night before, who had been enormously intrigued with the idea of the *Little Review*—did happen to be there. He took the detectives with him to some important city office and persuaded the powers that I was a flighty society girl who meant nothing she said. I discovered this later, after I had sat in the studio for two days patiently waiting for the detectives to come back.

*   *   *   *   *   *

And now we were very poor. Subscriptions kept coming in but advertising had fallen off on account of anarchism. We had taken a cheaper studio in the Fine Arts Building—room 834 on the Renaissance court where the fountain and the pianos tinkled all day.

At the right moment in October a friend on the *New Republic* asked if he couldn't present the *Little Review* with its annual trip to New York. The *Little Review* accepted with alacrity.

This charming man (whom I will call Jack), knowing that I had yet to hear my first performance of "Tristan

75

and Isolde," suggested that I arrive in New York on a certain Saturday morning. He would meet my train, take me to lunch and from there to the Metropolitan for Tristan with Toscanini and Fremstad. The prospect almost unnerved me.

Toscanini conducted the prelude with tears running down his face. Fremstad was the ideal Isolde; I was the ideal audience: I was stunned.

Afterward we went to tea (I was striding the high peaks of the Austrian Tyrol—an exercise I had read that Fremstad found necessary after singing Isolde). Jack had some friends I must know. They too had been to "Tristan." But they didn't look it. When they joined us with nonchalant faces I knew there was something wrong with them.

The man had intense red hair and a long body.

May I present the most rigorously informal man I know? asked Jack. Sinclair Lewis. He hasn't written anything yet but he will one day astonish America.

"Red" Lewis and his fiancée were completely informal about Tristan.

We tried to make an experience of it, said Lewis. We held hands but we couldn't manage to be moved.

Later Lewis came to Chicago and we did our best to be friends. But we couldn't communicate across the chasms that separated us. He was always attacking my standards for the *Little Review*.

76

You're too remote from the common herd, you believe in art for art's sake, you ought to be interested in the psychology of the average person as well as that of the exceptional person.

I am always so bored by this argument that I ignore it. I tried to make him talk of himself instead. He is an amusing and ardent person, condemned to perpetual vitality. He wouldn't be sidetracked. He wanted to talk about his barber and prove his theory. He had just come from his barber and told me a story about him on which I found it hard to fix my attention. I insisted that the only interest in the story was Sinclair Lewis' interest in telling it.

No, he said, that barber *is* interesting. It's your limitation that you don't 'see' him.

He told me that a certain man was in love with me.

Yes, I said, I know it.

But you refused him.

Yes, I know that too.

You don't care for him?

No. That's why I refused him.

But—well, I thought I'd like to talk to you about it, if I may, because I know he really cares for you.

Well?

I thought perhaps you didn't know.

Oh yes, I know.

That didn't make you care for him at all?

Should it?

Well, it often does.

It doesn't with me.

77

But how do you know?

Because it didn't.

But no, be serious with me.

I'm serious but the conversation doesn't seem to me enlightened.

Now just a moment. What I want to say is that perhaps you don't know yourself yet. That's the way it was with my wife and myself. We didn't fall in love at first sight. But when she found I cared for her and I found she cared for me—well, that made all the difference. We discovered that we were in love.

But I'm not like that.

Not like what?

So—long, shall we say, in finding things out.

But I'm telling you we thought we weren't like that either. And you see we were.

But I'm not.

How can you be sure?

Because I've never been.

But. . . .

My limitation? Or is life at such levels interesting?

This type of conversation left me without any curiosity about "Main Street," published a year or two later. I knew that "Main Street" contained none of the things I wanted to find out about life. I didn't read it until five years after its publication, in a mountain village in the Pyrenees, where I found it on the reading table of an inn. I sat up all night with it in an accumulative rage. Could this be the book that had caused an outcry in recognition of its art? There is no art in it. Its photography is faithful and insignificant. Its truth is unimportant. Faithful photography has never been a proof of art—nor has faithful psychology. The psychology of "Main Street's" people is representative, not special. Is it possible that anyone, everyone, should have compared it to Madame Bovary? Madame Bovary wasn't representative. She was different from every other woman in her town. Lewis' heroine is like every other woman in her town—she is merely a little more so. She is made of the same stuff as the rest of them. All of which can be traced to Lewis' theory that everyone is like everyone else, that everyone is interesting. No great book has ever been built on such a premise. A great book is always based upon the difference between its protagonist and the other characters—that is, the difference between the author and the other human beings he knows. The critics called "Main Street" a tragedy. It has no tragedy. Tragedy is . . . the difference.

* * * * * *

I came back from the New York Tristan and advertising campaigns with a number of good advertisements, but Chicago firms refused to contribute their quota. Marshall Field and Company was obdurate because it saw no reason to support an art magazine which didn't send it

79

thousands of customers. I found this so ungracious that I decided upon a gracious revenge. In the Christmas number I donated a page to every firm that should have advertised and didn't—a full page with a box in the centre, stating why that particular concern should have recognized us. James Howard Keelher, Chicago's publicity expert of the moment, congratulated me on the trick.

It's a genial idea, he said. Now go and collect money for the free publicity. They won't refuse you.

But they did. And I was left with a disdain of the business man's sense of humor.

* * * * * *

At Christmas time Lois appeared in Chicago with her two exceptional children—Tom who resembled Pan, and Fritz who looked like Von Hindenburg. Lois was bored with her husband's self-importance, had decided to divorce him and support herself and the children by taking a position on the *Little Review!*

It seemed that Swinburne had given way to Kipling. And the husband was so pleased with his manner of reading aloud that he often forgot and read the same story twice. Lois, sitting quietly through the second perusal, would then tell him. Since he always found time to lift his eyebrow in heavy reflection over the same passages, Lois felt he might have found time (they never do, I believe) to reflect that he was boring her. The result of this lack of perception was her flight to Chicago with all her household goods. The apartment forthwith became a most livable place—and we could no longer afford to live in it.

I wanted to find something modest in the country. And found it—going out at random on the Chicago and Northwestern and getting off at a station whose name promised much: Lake Bluff. There were two houses on the lake—lakes still being essential. Both could be rented for twenty-five dollars a month. One was lovely, much too large and without heating facilities. The other was small, practical and had a good furnace. We unhesitatingly took the former.

Everything was moved out to Lake Bluff, including the Mason and Hamlin grand piano. We enjoyed the luxury of the house and tried to keep warm around a vast fireplace in which wood showed no intention of burning. Alexander Berkman came out to spend a few days with us. Berkman was astonishing. His youth and vitality made it almost impossible to believe that he had spent fourteen years in prison, six of them in solitary confinement. The first night he told us prison stories as we huddled around the fire—stories so agonizing that some of them were not included in his book, "Prison Memoirs of an Anarchist." The next morning he announced he couldn't stay any longer—the house was too Siberian for him.

We decided that the other house might indeed be better. The Mason and Hamlin was moved again and we settled down to organized domestic life with a furnace. We had a negress, Clara Crane, who served in the double capacity of cook and nursemaid. She had a small son, Johnny, an

81

expert in clogging. Our organized domesticity consisted in song and dance furnished by Clara upon request at mealtime, and in Johnny's teaching Tom and Fritz to clog. Jean decided to be housekeeper and spent the time filling the rooms with pine branches. Harriet tramped the winter woods in induced melancholy. Lois received the camp-followers who invaded the studio, leaving my time free for editorial (anarchistic) writing. I played the Mason and Hamlin until three in the morning and slept on an uncovered balcony, usually waking under a blanket of snow.

We continued to be poor. Groceries could be charged but studio rent couldn't. Mr. Curtis, the Englishman who presided over the destinies of the Fine Arts Building, sent Mr. Greene on the futile mission of collecting the rent.

We really must have a check, poor Mr. Greene would insist.

You really want a check? And upon his repeated assurance of how sincerely he wanted it, I would write out a check for thirty dollars. A day or two later Mr. Greene would come back, embarrassed.

There's evidently some mistake. The bank says this check is not good.

But I didn't say it was good, I would answer, unembarrassed.

Mr. Greene's embarrassment mounted but his patience never diminished.

The printer howled for money. I sent him, in an elab-

orate envelope, all the money we had at the moment—
five cents. He didn't quite know what to say, what to do.

*   *   *   *   *   *

Emma Goldman, returning to Chicago, was ambitious
to lecture in the Fine Arts Building. There was a hall on
the tenth floor in which she felt she could attract a different type of audience for lectures on the drama. She was increasingly addicted to "art" and loved to talk on Shaw,
Ibsen, Tolstoy, Strindberg, Hauptmann. A Chicago business man had somehow become interested and saw the
possibility of her making a sensation in such a setting—
felt that Chicago society would willingly pay to be in-
sulted by Emma Goldman, the super-anarchist, if she
really would be super. He offered to rent the hall for a
series of ten lectures and to provide an intensive publicity.
I talked with Mr. Curtis and it was arranged. Emma
Goldman was at last announced on Michigan Boulevard.

The first lecture instead of being properly red and de-
nunciatory was probably the tamest of Emma Goldman's
career. She was irked by having a backer—an unknown
element in her life—and unconsciously toned down to
what she thought a "society" audience would want. Society wasn't thrilled and wouldn't come again. E. G.
felt that her backer was disappointed and returned the
money he had spent.

Lucian Cary who had succeeded Floyd Dell on the
Evening Post and whose talent was to write book reviews
like Lytton Strachey biographies in miniature, spoke of

Emma Goldman as "a nice woman with ideas less radical than Emerson's and certainly less interesting."

All this was distressing. We tried to make her see that she should have treated her audience roughly, but she wouldn't accept this idea. She wept. We were contrite but explained the psychology of insult—that such people got a kick out of being shown up for what they were. She couldn't imagine why. She thought they would be ashamed to hear what they were. At this point I felt a dim stirring in the brain—the first—that something was wrong; that if you spent your life talking to people about their faults and offering them panaceas, it might be just as well to find out something about them first.

I published an article in the L.R. to the effect that it was permissible to be sentimental about flowers or kittens or candy, but that to be sentimental about people was puerile. E.G. didn't approve of the article. She believes in people—she blames society, governments, institutions, for everything. She still feels this way to-day. Only a few months ago I asked her what was her present attitude, thinking that perhaps the years might have changed her philosophy. But not at all. Her eyes turned a deeper blue and she said tragically:

Anarchism is stronger than I am. I can't see people suffering without feeling I will die if I can't help them.

This attitude is obviously one of identification. For although she gives the impression of being able to stand anything, there are any number of things she can't stand. She can't stand wearing a fur coat—the thought of the murdered animal would suffocate her. She can't stand food that has been cooked by inexpert hands—she will go hungry rather than eat it. She can't stand small handkerchiefs, certain colors, many perfumes, flowers in a room at night. She can't stand reporters' questions. She can't stand being spoken to ungently. She can't stand references to money. I once addressed affectionately as our "angel" a man who had helped to bring out a number of the L.R. She was deeply shocked, found it vulgar. Of course the things she *can* stand needn't be entered into here.

I was particularly impressed by the fact that she couldn't stand the soft lapping of the lake outside our apartment. . . .

I made a joke for her: If the world only knew what a prima donna Emma Goldman is!

She laughed—but she couldn't quite stand that either.

*   *   *   *   *   *

Spring came on again. . . . The lilacs were in bloom, the lake was blue. From the bluff where our latest home had its foundations and its furnace we could look down through trees and wild flowers at the strip of yellow sand and water. And we had no money at all, not even the monthly twenty-five dollars.

One day, feeling that inspiration was demanded of me and that it was about to descend, I went exploring. The lake was beneficent, summer would come . . . what might not happen? I left the train at Ravinia, walked east and south along the shore toward Braeside. Between the bluff and the water's edge there was a wider strip of beach and no summer colony on the heights as at Lake Bluff. For at least a mile to the north there was no sign of humanity. At that extremity was Ravinia (symphony concerts in the summer); at the other, Braeside, within easy walking distance (trains to Chicago). . . . I needed no agency to point out to me that this place was clearly indicated as a summer residence. The only lack was the residence. But was this an essential obstacle? Wasn't camping a passion with all sensible people? What was to prevent our putting up tents and living the pristine life of nomads?

Nothing: except what I have always found the greatest drawback to doing anything in life—the necessity to explain your plans to others, hoping they will seize your meaning the first time. They don't.

I remember I sat gazing at the camp site and wondered if I had the strength to return to Lake Bluff, present the idea, hear the thud that follows non-acceptance, carefully pull the slower brains into my momentum—argue, explain, illustrate, stimulate, excite, until (after hours thus vividly spent) the "family" would begin to concede that I wasn't crazy. If anyone should ever ask me what I consider the most wearing experience known to mankind—which no one will, knowing that I lie in wait for such questions—I will answer: waiting for other people to act upon what I see.

I sat on the beach and planned the details. Then, having enjoyed the sunset and having pushed the train back

86

to Lake Bluff with my entire visceral system, I arrived as the family were dining on the porch by candlelight. I arranged my face (from the inside), composed my manner, reduced my tempo and asked them not to speak until I had projected an idea.

It went as badly as any pure inspiration has ever gone. No one (not even Lois who was usually so receptive) could see anything attractive or achievable in the plan. In the first place we couldn't get permission to camp on the beach. Second it would be dangerous at night. Third it presented the maximum of inconveniences. I answered that the greatest inconvenience I knew was paying rent; that there would be no danger if we had four or five tents with Clara as guardian; and as to asking permission, who had imagined asking anything?

We would simply take possession and it would be difficult to move us.

No one appreciated these distinctions. Jean announced that she was tired of a bohemian life and thought she would marry. Lois said Tom and Fritz needed no change —they were quite healthy where we were. I answered that the plan was not exclusively for health (though who had better health than gypsies?) We couldn't stay where we were—I had tapped all the resources I possessed and couldn't continue writing checks in the void. Harriet was hesitant because she still hoped to knock someone's block off and thus acquire the money to remain in the Lake Bluff house. So I had to sleep (or rather, not sleep) on failure. I went to bed only after announcing that it was the best plan ever born in a human brain and that it was certain to be carried out.

After lying awake, frustrated and mangled, I redoubled my efforts in the morning. I became so persuasive that they couldn't hold out. The things I found to say! One of them was I had an intuition we no longer needed a house. I felt one would be offered us when it became necessary. This happened—we were offered two. One offer was withdrawn before we could get into the house, but still . . . Life is beneficent if you insist upon its being so.

I explained that we would have five small tents with wood floors—one for Lois and the children, one for Harriet, one for me, one for Clara and Johnny and one for the kitchen. The first three would face the lake, the two latter would face each other, being joined by a floor which would serve as a dining room. When it rained we would eat in the kitchen. We would put in a stock of preserved food and bring fresh food from Chicago at night. We would roast corn over the camp fire, bake potatoes in the ashes. We would swim in the early morning, by moonlight, have great camp fires, coffee and bacon for breakfast . . . live in fact a North Shore gypsy life.

We did it. We were established by the middle of May and we stayed (some of us) until the middle of November. I remember because I took my last swim on November 14.

Each tent had a soldier's cot, a deck chair, an oriental rug. The tents were cheap. The wood for the floors cost only nine dollars. We had no moving expenses except the cartage on an overloaded truck from Lake Bluff to the beach. I was amused by the idea of testing our physical strength, so Harriet and I carried the household goods down the bluff. I had never before experienced the surcease that comes after doing more than one is able physically to do. We carried loads before which men would have hesitated. We placed floor boards and nailed them solidly together, pitched the tents, furnished them and had an enormous camp fire burning by the time the others arrived for dinner. It had taken all day.

We dined under the evening sky and slept under the stars—for by this time the gypsy band was so enthusiastic that all the cots were withdrawn from the tents and placed upon the sand.

The next six months were among the most lyrical of my life. I was at my worst—loving nature.

The days came and went. . . . For the first time I could employ this cliché with meaning. The days really did come and go. I watched them. They came up beneath my cot as I lay facing the east, and I left the studio in Chicago early enough to reach camp for the spectacle of the sunset and the beginning of night.

I was often up at sunrise. The first gesture of the day was to rush into a tent, change from pajamas to bathing suit, plunge into a cold lake, run on the beach. Then a fire of brushwood, a breakfast of coffee, bacon, fruit, an egg (if we were lucky). Then the ritual of the first morning cigarette, and then the ritual of dressing. At this point in the *Little Review's* fortunes I possessed one blouse, one hat and one blue tailored suit. The blouse could be made to serve two days. Then I washed it—by moonlight or by sunrise. Being of crêpe georgette it didn't need to be ironed. Somehow I managed to look well-dressed, continued to elicit those tributes without which I could not live: You look so beautifully groomed! It is just as well that people don't realize the secret of this matter. It lies chiefly in a manner of walking.

But it was difficult enough, considering that we were often overtaken by storms at night between the Braeside station and the camp. There was no shelter on the road. We accepted the rain as an adventure and splashed along the shore line. The storms were sometimes so violent, the blackness so overwhelming, that only in the flashes of lightning could we see to what depth we were wading in the lake. I would squeeze a few buckets of water from my suit, pat it gently into shape, hang it on a cord in my tent and go downtown the next morning looking immaculate. I remember these storms usually happened late at night, giving us an excuse for midnight swimming.

I remember above everything else the early evenings. Watching the day go became an obsession with me. I sat before my tent on my "porch" and looked and felt and heard with all my organism. So this is nature! was all I was capable of registering emotionally for six months.

Of course our idyl was not without its flaws—no idyl of my life has been.

First a policeman appeared to challenge our right to the property. I fought him rather too strenuously and saw the battle going against me. Desperation called forth an unknown force in my nature—the strategy of tact. I took him into my confidence, presented Tom and Fritz, contrasted their state of health and happiness with the tenement life which would be our fate if forced to leave the beach. He was Irish; he was moved. And we were not removed.

Lois soon deserted the camp for a second marriage and Harriet Dean and I were left alone. Cæsar came out to one of the empty tents. Of course we were subjected to a thousand annoyances. Reporters heard of us and featured us as a back-to-nature colony, a Hellenistic revival, a freak art group, a Nietzschean stronghold. . . . The *Tribune* made a full page Sunday story of us with photographs of the tents and quotations from my more infuriated repulsions of the reporters.

But it would have taken more than these minor vicissitudes to cool my ardor, and mother's hopes of breaking my spirit had never been more completely at a discount.

Ben Hecht and Maxwell Bodenheim walked out from Chicago and left poems pinned on my tent. Sherwood Anderson came to express his approval and to tell stories around the camp fire. Lucian Cary and I intoxicated ourselves on ideas. Lawrence Langner, who was organizing the New York Theatre Guild, came to extol group action and socialism . . . ineffectually, of course.

* * * * * *

Only one fantasy failed of accomplishment. I had planned to have the Mason and Hamlin shipped to the beach through the agency of some (non-existent) boat service. But no one would help me with this idea. No one seemed to feel it within the realm of those things one talked of so long as one retained one's sanity. So we had it moved into the Fine Arts studio instead, where it led to a musical adventure.

Among all the pianos we heard from our studio windows, there was one I listened to with critical pleasure. It was played by someone who had what I consider the essential requisite of piano playing—the orchestral line.

These sounds issued from the open windows of the Chase Piano Company on the fifth floor. The unknown pianist and I began playing back and forth and then I went to see who it was. I found a charming pale boy of seventeen named Allen Tanner. He looked as a modern pianist should look—short hair closely modeled to the head, well-cut conventional clothes, a decorative body used with rigid economy in relation to his instrument. We became friends (and enemies) for life—the condition of enmity being produced by his gift for interpreting my words to mean anything but what I say.

He attached himself to the *Little Review* and its foibles, played the "Love Death" for the anarchists at gala gatherings (where they chanted his genius so loudly they couldn't hear his playing), took Emma Goldman to performances of "Pelléas and Melisande" and played for me so continuously that the time would have to be reckoned in years.

The Chase Company employed him because he was one of those people who really know how to touch a piano. He could make any piano sound like a Mason and Hamlin. He still can—even French pianos—beyond which nothing need be said. And since he has besides "the most beautiful voice in the world" (a voice of the same type as his piano playing), he is living in misery in Paris—probably the only example left on earth of the artist who knows nothing of being a business man. Allen should be maintained in magnificence as a court pianist, if Renaissance courts could be revived. As it is, he wears his life out trying to make life decorative enough to be endured. He has three qualities to the degree of genius—his musical ear (he accurately transcribed Scriabine's "Poem d'Extase" to the piano after one hearing of Stowkowski's orchestral reading), his incomparable legato playing, and the art of standing in his own light. He can do this so well that one feels he will never relinquish the gift.

At this point of the *Little Review's* adventures in the seven arts I was most propelled toward the art of music. I was at a climax of piano worship. Incited to lyric madness by the Imagists, I composed for the L.R. three

pages of sound and color combinations made up from
their poetry and supposed to represent the state which
the modern piano should attain. John Gould Fletcher
and others who should have known better wrote me
that this was really good stuff. So I continued. We
were still in the good old days when all the arts were
striving to approach the condition of painting, so I could
do my worst—though I remember glimmerings of a certain native good sense which made me, in another pan-
egyric, go in for form rather than for color. I wrote an
article about Harold Bauer, asking why pianists didn't
renounce playing the Lizst Campanella—that it should be
impossible for a modern pianist to do that kind of thing.
Bauer responded with a charming letter in which he said
that I had been profoundly intuitive—that he was in fact
unable to play the Campanella, that he always had been,
and that he would like to know the editor of the *Little
Review*.

On his next visit to Chicago we met through a friend
who had a Fine Arts Studio with a surplus of attractive
objects—two Mason and Hamlin grand pianos.

Bauer was the most interested person I had yet known.
He was passionately and precisely interested in everything
—above all in the idea behind everything. This gave him a
curiously intense attention. He would talk of Schoenberg's
new piano music, Amy Lowell's poetry, Freud's new
psychoanalysis, the building of bridges, the modern
painters, the human comedy. . . . He had been so interested in piano mechanism that he had learned to build a

piano. He always had his piano hammers broadened and blunted for deep sound, rather than sharpened and pointed for brilliant sound, as Gabrilowitsch preferred. He used the lightest possible action. He loved the Mason and Hamlin above any other piano.

We had tea and went for a long walk, talking avidly. We walked north along Michigan Boulevard to the river, sections of the city which he found very fine. His talk was always pointed by a delicate irony, though, as he said, irony was the quality his managers were always hoping he would eliminate from his public life.

He told a story of a concert in Seattle. The hall was filled with a music-loving but boisterous audience, including children, bent on refreshing itself with candy and peanuts. When he sat down at the piano he could hear nothing but the cracking of shells. He broke off playing, approached the footlights and made a gracious speech, saying that he felt he was making a great noise and interrupting the audience; he would retire to the wings and come back later to play. When he came on a second time the silence was complete. After the concert he was visited by a group of people—a group with the unmistakable look of a delegation. They wished to assure Mr. Bauer that he had been laboring under a false impression, that he had not interrupted them.

After our promenade we came back to the two pianos. Bauer sat down at one of them and began to play, as if it were of no great consequence to anyone to hear Harold Bauer play in private. Afterward he asked me to dine and

I, being more of an adolescent than I have perhaps yet indicated in these pages, refused, saying I had proofs to read—not during his concert that evening, naturally, but during dinner.

But you can't work all the time, said Bauer, no proofs can be so important as that.

I explained that we were going to press and that the proofs must be done by morning. He felt I wasn't telling the truth. He became a little chilled. A look of remoteness passed across his eyes, as if he were taking himself away from the situation.

I hadn't told the truth. The truth was that I didn't want to dine with him. Two inhibitions were already fixed upon me—two complexes characteristic of the American sensibility: first, I had to be alone in order fully to realize the wonders of the afternoon; second, I was afraid I might not be interesting at dinner. And who could survive the agony of such a catastrophe?

Bauer came often to Chicago where he had devoted and fervent audiences. Sometimes enroute he would telegraph me to lunch or dine and talk. I was less self-conscious as the years went by and always accepted in haste. Once we fought half the night about Isadora Duncan's dancing— he being enormously interested in it as art, I being totally uninterested in it as sex. I wrote an article trying to prove that dancing was to Isadora as catnip to the cat—that she was good "art material" (as proved by the innumerable good sketches painters made of her), but that she hadn't "the fragile mighty thing." Bauer couldn't see it that way. I never found more than one or two people who could. And now that Isadora has died so picturesquely one of those two will certainly have changed her opinion. The other is a person whose opinions endure. Her name is Jane Heap. She will appear later in this book.

The most interesting conversation I had with Harold Bauer was about piano playing. He had begun life as a violinist, in London. But one day he had an opportunity to make some money if he would accept the rôle of pianist in a trio which was to tour Europe.

I knew nothing of the piano, he said, I had merely observed pianists. I consulted a professor who assured me I could play the piano if I would place myself in his hands and do nothing but scales for six months. But that didn't help me to play on Saturday afternoon. If I didn't I would lose the job. I decided that my intelligence was equal to the situation. I had often taken my sister to Letchititsky's studio, where she was studying, and what I heard there as the fundamentals of piano playing didn't seem to me interesting. From my observation I had remarked that pianists sat back in their chairs with an authoritative air when they wanted to play powerfully or loudly, and that they sat cherishingly over their instruments when they wanted to play softly. I figured that if I could make the dynamics of this hold true from the shoulder down to the finger-tip, if I could inform the body, the whole length of arm, with my intention I would have found the secret. So I began to play the piano that way.

In other words, said the person of enduring opinions who was present, you applied a second art to the art of piano playing.

What do you mean? asked Bauer.

You applied the art of the actor to the art of the pianist.

Why, yes, exactly, said Bauer. A very good definition. I have really done nothing but that. My playing began on that basis. Development is inevitable. I play differently to-day from the way I played a year ago. Next year I will play differently still. But I have used no other theory. It is a theory of good sense.

We discussed the more complicated questions of inspiration, of putting across one's emotions, of making happen before an audience those things that happen so easily in one's own room.

There is always a moment at the beginning of a concert, Bauer went on, when one waits for the mechanism to adjust itself perfectly to the preconceived idea. Until this adjustment takes place the poor pianist is the most miserable of creatures. I sometimes play for ten minutes before it happens. I call in vain upon my resources; I tell myself how interested I am in the music I'm playing; I try to remember how interested Chopin must have been when he composed the passages that feel like lead under my fingers. But nothing helps until that magical moment when the clogs of the machine seem to slip into place. . . .

People are often amusing in their misconceptions of what the artist is doing and feeling. Once a man congratulated Harold Bauer on a passage in Cæsar Franck's Prelude Chorale and Fugue.

I'm glad to see, Mr. Bauer, that you play all the notes of that passage in the bass. So many pianists blur them.

My dear sir, replied Bauer, I didn't play them at all. I purposely leave them out. The passage sounds better that way.

Paderewski, examining the hands of a Bauer pupil and finding none of the Letchititsky development, would shake his head sadly. But Bauer is no respecter of systems.

How shall I finger this passage, Mr. Bauer? a new pupil asked.

How do I know? Bauer answered. *I* would finger it like this. You, having a different hand, will obviously finger it differently. It will depend on your idea of the passage. First tell me your idea. . . .

* * * * * *

But to get back to camp—this being a war story.

In the early days of September, I was exploring the Highland Park beach when I came upon an empty house, situated high on the bluff and of such a perfect romanti-

99

cism that it occurred to me we should live in it. It was of the cottage type, painted a faded gray with a white trim, and it was probably the most sympathetic house anyone has ever seen. There is always a delicate way of breaking into abandoned houses, so I examined this one thoroughly and found it the ideal home. Every room had an old fireplace, every window had the lake. I made our winter plans. There was the perfect driveway culminating in a long side porch where Tom and Fritz would arrive in the snow for an old-fashioned Christmas. There was the perfect dining room for the Yule log and the feast. There was the perfect surrounding forest for the pine and cedar and evergreen branches. There was the perfect old kitchen for the mince-meat pies. . . .

It was too good to believe, but we acquired the house.

I learned that it belonged to a Mr. and Mrs. Buckley who had built a mansion near by, preserving the old homestead out of tenderness. Harriet and I called upon Mrs. Buckley, presenting our plan with great fantasy and charm—or so we hoped. And so it seemed. Mrs. Buckley responded with an almost maternal sympathy and appeared thrilled at the prospect of renting her house to us for nothing a year, if we would put in our own furniture, and if we were sure to be comfortable and happy in it. There remained only to see her husband for his sanction. She promised to talk to him that night and I could call upon him at his offices the next day. She offered us chocolates and tea and we parted like old friends. The next day I saw Mr. Buckley who added to his permission the offer of a large kitchen range to keep us warm in the most rigorous weather.

I can mark this moment as one of the happiest of my life, and I hope that Mr. and Mrs. Buckley are alive and that they read these pages. I shall never forget that Sunday morning in camp when Harriet and Cæsar started off triumphantly to begin the installation and returned tragically to announce that Mrs. Buckley had appeared and said that if I were the Margaret Anderson who was camping on the beach and being written about in the papers she wouldn't think of giving her house to such a person. Harriet tried to convince her that I wasn't such a person, and I suppose tried to convert her to anarchism in the same breath—and made no headway as Mrs. Buckley kept repeating that it had been a great shock to her to discover that anyone who appeared so charming could be so depraved.

I renounced the house without a struggle. We didn't think of using our brains. I might have gone back to see Mrs. Buckley, convinced her that my father and mother were so and so, that I was so and so, that I was just as "charming" as I seemed, that I had never been "such a person." It never occurred to me. Losing that house and all the projects connected with it—(and who knows what eternal legend might not have adhered to the name of Buckley for having sheltered the *Little Review!*) seemed to me the inevitable price one pays for having an ideal. I sat gazing at the sea (lake) torn between the glory of martyrdom and the pain of losing a house. If it had only been a fortune or a diamond mine that I was asked to renounce. But a house! To one of my intense inter-uterine nature there is no measuring the shock that the loss of a house can cause.

We didn't know what to do but to go on camping. October was passing and I was wondering what sort of arctic preparations we could make to meet the North Shore winter when a man named Wentworth (a socialist we had met at the Emma Goldman lectures) wrote that he had a vacant house on Indiana Avenue which he would be glad to place at our disposal. We accepted and decorated as for a life tenancy. As there was a music room we installed the Mason and Hamlin. But the Buckley disaster had been too much for me—I couldn't put any first-rate enthusiasm into Indiana Avenue. And I believe Mr. Wentworth had some vague hope that his house would become the nucleus for socialist-anarchist debates. As I still had a horror of collective activities I carefully evaded any such development.

At this moment the most interesting thing that had happened to the *Little Review*—the most interesting thing that ever happened to it—took place in February. Jane Heap appeared. . . .

JANE HEAP

There is no one in the modern world whose conversation I haven't sampled, I believe, except Picasso's. So I can't say it isn't better than Jane Heap's. But I doubt it in spite of his reputation. I felt in 1916 and feel to-day that Jane Heap is the world's best talker.

It isn't a question of words, facility, style. It isn't a question of erudition. It isn't even a question of truth. (Who knows whether what she says is true?) It is entirely a question of ideas. No one can find such interesting things to say on any subject. I have often thought I should like to give my life over to talk-racing, with my money on Jane. No one else would ever win—you can't win against magic. What it is exactly—this making of ideas—I don't know. Jane herself doesn't know.

Things become known to me, she says.

She talks usually in monosyllables, with here and there an important word placed so personally as to give it a curious personal significance. It is impossible to quote her. You can hear that done, with appropriate disaster, by anyone who tries it. I will try.

Take a group of people discussing sophistication, for

example. You hear every possible definition of sophistication—you already know them all. Then Jane says:

A really sophisticated person? I should say a person who is used to being a human being.

You are discussing Debussy, perhaps, with people who knew him.

I have never seen Debussy, Jane says. I have seen a photograph or two and I know of course that he died of cancer. I should say it's certain he had a tumor on the brain. That explains his look—the eyes pushed out from the inside, the head pushed forward; a body built for strength and violence, from which all the strength had been drained. His music is a striking example of the 'tumorous' school of art.

Or Chaliapin:

Chaliapin's school of gestures might be classed under secondary feminine traits. There is the 'grace' of the hands, but it is the feet that are the most distinctive thing about the man—walking from the knee with short steps, the narrow base, constantly shifting and turning on the heels, producing an effect of complete harmlessness. In the death scene (Boris) the feet lie like a dead canary's.

Or you are discussing Lytton Strachey's Elizabeth and Essex. Why did Elizabeth do this, why did Essex do that?

Elizabeth and Essex, Jane says, are one of the great cases of alter-ego. That's why Elizabeth could not have him go on living after her. That's why Essex (passive to her active) could accept his death from her.

Strachey records a wealth of psychological data. He

gives no indication, on any page of his book, that he knew he was dealing with the particular psychology of the alter-ego and with no other.

Or take James Joyce's Exiles—a play written in Joyce's young manhood and never presented, I believe, except with indifferent success in New York. Joyce knew exactly with what psychology he was dealing: (himself). But no reader quite knows. I have listened to at least a hundred misinterpretations. Jane can illuminate:

There are people, a few, always the artist I should say, who inspire such strong love in all who know them that these in turn become inspired by love for one another. The truth of the matter is that such a person is neither loved nor lover but in some way seems to be an incarnation of love, possessing an eternal element and because of it a languor, a brooding, a clair-voyance of life and a disdain. In other people he breeds a longing akin to the longing for immortality. They do not love him: they become him. Richard is one of these.

There is much talk of freedom in the play. Everyone wanting everyone else to be free, it is shown that there is at no time any freedom for anyone. The discussion of the wife's decision when she went away with Richard—unasked by him—proves she has no freedom to make a decision. She may have been in love with Robert, but she had no choice: she was Richard. Robert is in love with Richard, has always been; but he is an unthinking natural man. He follows nature with his brain and thinks he is in love with Richard's wife, a woman being the conventional symbol for a man's love. But when he has a meeting with her and they are left alone by Richard in perfect freedom they are foiled, they are both Richard, both trying to reach Richard, not each other. Richard's old conflict with his mother (just indicated) was based on her refusal to become him. The wife sees the child going the way of all of them.

There is nowhere in the world for Richard to turn for love. Sex as other men know it can be for him only a boring, distasteful need of the body. Love strikes back at him from every source. His becomes a Midas tragedy.

He is tormented by the commonplace 'beaten path' love-making of Robert and his wife. He asks her infinite questions; he directs the love-making to save his sensibilities. He says to Robert: "Not like this—this is not for people like us." Yet he wishes darkly that they had dishonoured him in a common, sneaking way. Not that he cares for either of them, not that he cares for honour or for conventions, but then he might have been free of them. They would have acted for once without his spirit having been the moving force.

A phrase of Jane's I have always remembered was one she found as a tribute to someone who (briefly) understood her: A hand on the exact octave that is me. Another was for a person whom everyone considered dramatic and exceptional: If what you say of B. seems true to you, then all my ideas are meaningless. B. is a stereotyped person, oblivious of drama going on about him. Why should a person hold to his one little facet when to have many facets is the plan—cut like a diamond, a face for every environment. An actor, that is the idea.

This was the kind of perception I liked. Jane's impersonal judgment of people was always unexpected—and always creative. I decided that it must be presented in the *Little Review*.

106

Jane Heap's arrival on the *Little Review* was not unaccompanied by drama. The magazine was two years old when she was brought to the studio one day—by whom I've forgotten. The camp followers were there *en masse*, among them an erratic rich woman with a high temper who was considering giving us some money—she had nineteen millions.

We were talking of Duse and D'Annunzio. The millionairess hated Fire, felt that D'Annunzio was ignoble to have exposed Duse to such intimate treatment. She worked up her theme with sentimental abandon.

Jane regarded her with interest and then gave a loud and tender laugh.

God love Duse, said Jane, she has always given me a large pain. . . .

Nineteen Millions was furious. She left the studio saying that she disliked frivolity. She had always felt that the *Little Review* was a sanctum one could depend on for serious and inspiring conversation.

My reaction was different. I felt that I could never henceforth dispense with Jane Heap's frivolity.

Jane and I began talking. We talked for days, months, years. . . . We formed a consolidation that was to make us much loved and even more loathed. We talked every place, to all sorts and conditions of people. I made up quarrels of opinion so that Jane could show her powers. I must have been insupportable. But here was my obsession

—the special human being, the special point of view. I never let anyone escape her psychological clairvoyance.

Jane of course didn't like it entirely.

It's an awkward rôle for me. You're the buzz and I'm the sting.

And she didn't at all share my obsession about enlightening the world.

Why should I care what people think? They should think the way they do. I've nothing to say to them. And I don't want them to know what *I* think. I believe in silence of the people, by the people and for the people.

This would send me into a panic. Imagine allowing the intellectuals to stagnate in stupidity when a word or two from her would change their mental life!

Sometimes Jane would revolt openly:

I'm perfectly relaxed, you know, about the intellectuals. They're getting on all right.

Sometimes we spent one of those relaxed evenings at the house of some intellectual moron, Jane affronting me by appearing to enjoy everything, laughing her richest laugh at all the ineptitudes that should have been corrected, leaving me exhausted with the faces I had made trying to force her to talk. Afterward:

Why wouldn't you talk?

I was having a good time.

Well, I wasn't. Do you think it's interesting to see you sitting there looking as if you didn't know the difference between a good opinion and a bad one?

Yes, I think it's interesting. I think it's quite a feat.

Later when Jane decided to join the *Little Review* I tried to make her write every month at least one of the things she had talked that month. This required the greatest effort I have ever put into anything. We always spent two or three days arguing about the necessity to instruct anyone on any subject.

I don't know where you get your interest in the people in Wyoming. Why should the L.R. tell them all these things? They don't want to hear them. I hate propaganda.

Why call it propaganda? You've got to have ideas in a magazine of creative opinion.

Why?

Well, what should be in it?

Nothing, that I can see.

You can't have a magazine without something in it.

Why have a magazine?

Finally after three days of these negations she was willing to admit that it was just as well as not to have a *Little Review*. Every month we went through this drama with the same intensity. Beginning with the statement that she had no interest in life, Jane would spend several hours regretting that condition of childhood in which the photographer held up the bird to catch one's attention. I would then offer the *Little Review* as a substitute for the photographer's bird. She would concede that it might be so. Following which I would establish that it was by far the most exciting bird that could be found.

After these struggles I was completely worn out, but I rallied inevitably at Jane's first relenting words.

I'm a talker, I'm no writer, she would groan in a rather hopeful tone—by which I knew that she was ready to begin an article.

The next effort then began. My technique consisted in locking the doors and assuring her that nothing would break her concentration for several days. I would do all the marketing—which was just as well in any case, as Jane disliked divulging to tradespeople the perfectly private matter of what food she was going to consume.

The process of encouraging her to put down on paper the things she said consisted, first, of reiterating the impossibility of such a feat; second, of regretting the lack of money which prevented us from installing a dictaphone; third, of assuring her I could take down her conversation in long hand; fourth, of convincing her that she needn't turn self-conscious about it; fifth, that—well, that everything would be wonderful.

Then we plunged into hours of psychological gossip, touching such a range of subjects that it was impossible to decide which one would be of greatest news value for the *Little Review*.

*   *   *   *   *   *

But we didn't begin this frenzy of writing until after California. California was an inspiration I had as I cast about, in a spring fever, for a solution to the summer.

There was to be no repetition of camping—I rarely attempt repetitions. I thought that great forests would offer the perfect contrast to tents on a beach. Our summer would be camping of a kind, no doubt—at least I hoped so —but the setting must change. When Nineteen Millions asked me to visit her in Mill Valley, California, I decided that we would all go.

Mill Valley is a small town in the mountains surrounding San Francisco. We would rent some sort of mountain cabin to live (talk) in, we could conduct the *Little Review* from San Francisco, and I could see Nineteen Millions at intervals. There may be millionaires with whom one is willing to spend more than intervals. I have never seen one. Except perhaps Otto Kahn. But then he too is a talker. . . .

I was by this time so insane with the mental satisfactions of Jane's presence that I had lost all social consciousness. In a letter to Mill Valley I announced that, happily, it was possible to have Jane Heap near for the summer and that I was bringing her with me. A telegram flashed back from Mill Valley:

Have never liked Jane Heap. Suggest you come alone as arranged.

This failed to register as definitely as if I hadn't been able to read. The fact that I was doing something *gauche* which normally would have filled me with distaste, failed to penetrate any portion of my talk-fevered brain. I forgave Nineteen Millions her deplorable lack of enthusiasm for Jane Heap. We would spend the first evening discussing Art from a new angle, and she would thank the destiny that had forced Jane upon her. I tore up her telegram. Ten minutes later I would have questioned its arrival. I said nothing of it to Jane. One could never be sure of Jane's accepting any invitation, even from people who solicited her presence as the most vital event in their lives.

California plans progressed. We put a sign on the studio door announcing our departure for the beginning of June. Inside we hung posters proclaiming the necessity of aid—clothes, food, donations. The public was intrigued, the response lavish—some fifteen pounds of candy, five or six cakes, baskets of fruit, packages of tea, coffee, cans of conserves, a choice of hats, gloves, lingerie. We had arranged by this time to earn our railroad fares, and I was to have three hundred dollars from my grandmother who had died without ever having heard of the *Little Review*. This money hadn't come yet but it was to follow me; and I was ready to start with only a ticket and five dollars. We were going tourist, on the Canadian Pacific. As to our living in California, we would have a subscription boom for the magazine which would help both it and us. And as to getting back, we would stop in Los Angeles and Denver (where we already had faithful followers) and collect enough subscriptions for the return fares.

Unbelievably, the tourist car was empty except for us. It wasn't hot, and my chronic blue suit was fairly comfortable. The porter was the best of his species and cooked our meals in one of the kitchenettes. Our delicacies held out until the end. Most of the five dollars held out. The only thing which didn't hold out was Cæsar's trousers. He had leapt from side to side of the train so enthusiastically, not wishing to miss any of the view, that the seat of his pants had given way under the strain. He sewed them up at regular intervals, but the last day he was forced to spend in his berth. In Vancouver, where we had a stop-over, he managed somehow to get from the train to a tailor, who patched him up. The trousers lasted as far as Mill Valley.

We arrived in Mill Valley after lunch and went directly to the house of Nineteen Millions, to greet her and to explain that we would stay at an inn until we could find some place to live. Of course I had a feeling that she had already changed her attitude, that she would exclaim: How wonderful to have the whole *Little Review* staff—especially Jane Heap. You must all stay with me—I have so little of interest in my life.

This kind of thing may sometimes happen to some people. It has never happened to me to have any enthusiasm of mine accepted with enthusiasm. Everyone begins immediately to assure me that I must be crazy. And I remark that when they accept the enthusiasm later, in terms as violent as my own, they always neglect to state that *they* must have been crazy.

Nineteen Millions wasn't at home. A maid explained that she had gone to San Francisco to meet my train. I said we would wait in the garden—it appeared to be vast.

So we went out and sat on a large hill from which we could watch the house. I was articulating the plans which N.M. would undoubtedly make, when I saw a bright green dress silhouetted against the porch. It was obviously N.M. back from the train. The silhouette was of such rigidity that Jane said,

Well, I guess we'll be going. . . .

No. Wait here until I come back.

I went to the porch and found a woman with a disagreeable face.

Wait just a moment, I said as a greeting, I'll be back to talk.

I went out to the hill again.

We leave here instantly. Go back to the station and find the cheapest inn. I'll join you in half an hour.

They went rollicking down the hill. . . . We had just a dollar and a half left in the world.

I went back to the house.

I never visit anyone who isn't overcome with pleasure to have me. So now that is settled and I'm going away, you may care to explain why you look so despondent.

It's inconceivable that you didn't know I wanted you to come alone.

I did know it. It didn't interest me. If I visit anyone at this time in my life I have a condition to impose.

You know I didn't accept that condition. Jane Heap is

odious to me. I can't imagine why you came thinking you could force her down my throat.

I didn't think I could. I only hoped so.

I don't know what you think you are, really.

Yes, you do. I think I'm interesting. That's why you wanted me to visit you. And I've found someone who is much more interesting than I am.

I have many interesting things in my life. I don't need suggestions from anyone as to what will interest me.

Oh, but I mean *interesting*. I doubt if you have anything that's really interesting. There's so little of it about. It has to be made. . . . And there are so few people who can make it. . . .

And I went on to develop my code of life—that she might not want to be interested but that it would be negligent of me not to try to make her want to be, that such was my mission in life. I have wondered since that she didn't strike me. I once saw her strike a man in the face simply because he wouldn't answer her. But then is there anything so exasperating as not being answered?

She was decidedly decent about our argument. So was I. Neither of us raised her voice. We contrasted our opposing points of view for half an hour, exchanged insults and regrets, and said good-by amicably.

Our next meeting was two years later when she came to see me on Long Island. Jane was there and felt like talking. She talked all day. When she finished N.M. said to me:

I've never heard anything like it. You must both come

and visit me in New York. But especially Jane. I hope you'll come of course but I *must* have Jane.

I was a bit put out. It seems to me I could have lived my life without antagonisms if I could always have slowed it down by about two years.

That afternoon in Mill Valley I went down the hill and found the others in a little hotel near the station—fifty cents each for the night. Cæsar had enough money left to go back to San Francisco and search a lodging. The next morning Harriet also went there because she had friends from whom she could borrow. They meant to find a studio for the *Little Review*. Jane and I started out to find a house in the mountains where we could talk, undisturbed, for five months.

CALIFORNIA

We looked everywhere and found nothing. The laws
that good conversation impose are exacting. You must
never consider any environment that looks new. There
must be an atmosphere of other lives upon it. If you can
find an abandoned house with a straggling garden you've
found perfection. And if you find, besides, a hill or a
mountain or a few great trees. . . .

Finding nothing at all in the immediate neighborhood
of Mill Valley we decided to take our lunch and walk
miles in any direction, trusting that something would
appear. Muir Woods appeared, and this marvel of nature
fixed our choice. Within a mile we came upon what we
wanted—a small ranch house placed quite alone with a
background of mountains and a foreground of eucalyptus
trees leading to the sea, three miles away. The ranch house
fulfilled all demands—it was old, simple, homely, deserted, isolated, sympathetic. It was painted an ugly
brown. It had a roofless porch, a glass-enclosed room at
the back, a grove of eucalyptus at the side, a rear gate and
fence worthy of a rodeo, and a barn. Jane found an un-
resisting window and we climbed in. There was a living
room, three small bedrooms and a kitchen—all papered

hideously. But it would be easy to neutralize the paper by painting the furniture the right colors.

We built a fire in the living room, had our tea, decided our color schemes and hastened back to Mill Valley to find the owner.

We discovered that our house belonged to a Mr. Chase, but our informants neglected to explain that he was the sheriff. So I sought him out without suspecting his authority and told him that we simply must have his ranch house for the summer.

Mr. Chase was a sandy-haired Englishman with long twisted mustaches and looked like a sheriff in the western movies. But he had an unmelodramatic and humorous eye.

How do you know you want my house? You haven't seen it inside.

Oh yes we have. We broke in.

He drew back his coat, exposing his star.

I'm the sheriff of Mill Valley. What am I going to do about such burglary?

What he did was uniquely satisfactory. He had promised the ranch for the summer to two old friends—the town tailor and his wife who needed country air. They were ready to move into it the next day. But Mr. Chase hurriedly withdrew this offer and we got the ranch. At the end of the summer the tailor, putting new touches to my old suit, confessed he hadn't liked us at first as we had done him out of a holiday. I was consternated. Mr. Chase hadn't told us—he had merely taken me to his bank (when I explained being without money), justified my dubious situation, insisted that they honor my check when it arrived, and rented the ranch to us for twelve dollars a month. I was to pay him sixty dollars in advance. If we left the house in good condition I was to receive twelve dollars back at the end of the season. Mr. Chase didn't suspect our talent with houses. . . . When he looked at his ranch in October he wanted to refund all the money. The furniture was painted so cleverly that the wall paper was invisible. The fireplace which had been the ugliest brown that exists was brilliant white with a red border. Before it sat two resurrected armchairs painted white, with cushions of green and white striped canvas. Outside the house Jane had built stationary tables and chairs and painted them an orange that blended with the gray-blue of the eucalyptus and the mud-beige of the California hills. All these embellishments we left to Mr. Chase. He deserved them. When Emma Goldman came out from San Francisco to visit us the situation might have become complicated. It was during an uprising against the anarchists in that city. Tom Mooney and some other quite innocent man had been thrown into prison— and were kept there I believe for several years—because someone had thrown a bomb during a parade. The anarchists were being watched and Emma Goldman's movements followed by the police. When she took a ferry-boat and then a train for Mill Valley the authorities tele-phoned to Mr. Chase.

Look out for Emma Goldman. She's gone to your town.

Yes, I know, answered poor Mr. Chase, she's visiting in my house.

*   *   *   *   *   *

We moved to the ranch before my check came. Jane began on the furniture and I set out to find the necessary grand piano.

There was a Mason and Hamlin agency in San Francisco. I visited it but without the usual success. There were very few grand pianos on the coast, those few were always taken for concerts or rented at exorbitant rates, they hadn't one they could rent even if I could have paid their price; they certainly couldn't consider giving me one. It looked like a dead-lock so I sat down to compose a letter to Mr. Mason, head of the firm in Boston. I had never seen Mr. Mason but I assumed that he must know of my Mason and Hamlin passion, as exposed in the *Little Review*. I explained that since it was my intention to become one of the world's most beautiful pianists and since the Mason and Hamlin was the world's most beautiful piano, I didn't see how I could live without one for a whole summer. Could he tolerate such a situation?

I posted the letter without much hope of a result and went back to the ranch trying to think of other plans should that one fail.

My check came. We went into Mill Valley, paid Mr. Chase sixty dollars, stocked up with provisions, carried them to the ranch in knapsacks strapped on our backs, put our house in order, went into San Francisco to inspect and rent a studio Cæsar had found in the Montgomery Building, and explored the city—especially Chinatown, where we bought bright red Chinese lacquer bowls for twenty-five cents and handsome strips of Chinese gold, red, orange and green paper for walls and tablecloths. . . . The charm of San Francisco will always be concentrated for me in little red lacquer bowls.

Back on the ranch again, immersed in carpentry and decoration, I was unprepared for the arrival of a long envelope with Mason and Hamlin engraved in blue in the corner.

I have read your letter with much pleasure, wrote Mr. Mason—(why did I save so few letters?)—and I will ask you to go into San Francisco, choose the Mason and Hamlin BB which pleases you most, and have it sent out to your ranch at my expense. . . .

He followed this with thanks for my loyalty, hopes for my pianistic future, felicitations on my being able to put over to him an emotional attitude about his pianos. (In case it isn't generally known the BB is a concert grand—the largest made.)

Fortunately the house was equal to it. We gave it one side of the living room and I used this for my studio. Jane took the glass-enclosed room and made it into a combination carpentry shop and painter's atelier. (I've neglected to say that Jane began life at sixteen as a painter. That is why she talks so well. When painters are really good at talking they are better than anyone else.)

* * * * * *

I practiced in the morning. Our talk began with luncheon, reached a climax at tea, and by dinner we were staggering with it. By five o'clock in the morning we were unconscious but still talking. Chiefly we talked ART—not "æsthetically" (no talk is so callow) but humanely. We talked of the human being behind the art manifestation—what had made him, what was the distinguishing mark, the "strange necessity." In other words we talked psychology—a kind of prelude to behaviorism, a speculation concerning "beyond behaviorism." My mind was inflamed by Jane's ideas because of her uncanny knowledge of the human composition, her unfailing clairvoyance about human motivation. This was what I had been waiting for, searching for, all my life.

Jane and I were as different as two people can be. Temperamentally we were almost never in accord, intellectually we had taken different routes. I was full of borrowed information. I quoted philosophers and poets. Jane never quoted anyone except sometimes a great poet. She had to say everything in a personal way. She couldn't say anything that she hadn't made up herself.

The result of our differences was—argument. At last I could argue as long as I wanted. Instead of discouraging Jane, this stimulated her. She was always saying that she never found enough resistance in life to make talking worth while—or anything else for that matter. And I had always been confronted with people who found my zest for argument disagreeable, who said they lost interest in any subject the moment it became controversial. My answer had been that argument wasn't necessarily controversy. What could they know of either since it was their instinct instantly to shut off both? I had never been able to understand why people dislike to be challenged. For me challenge has always been the great impulse, the only liberation.

This book so far may have given the impression that I have had no difficulty in making myself, that I sprang like a warrior out of the earth. If so, I have been unjust to my effort. I wasn't born to be a fighter. I was born with a gentle nature, a flexible character and an organism as equilibrated as it is judged hysterical. I shouldn't have been forced to fight constantly and ferociously. The causes I have fought for have invariably been causes that should have been gained by a delicate suggestion. Since they never were, I made myself into a fighter. Once you start such an idea you find that it creeps up on you. I remember periods when I have been so besieged that I had to determine on a victory a day in order to be sure of surviving. I can still find among old papers lists written out—in ink —of fights that had to be won during the week or never. My life has been a "Penman's Progress"—I have made so many lists.

Four times the progress has been almost too difficult.

123

Four times I feared I could not win. First, when I broke away from home; second, when I gave my ultimatum to mother; third, when I struggled out of a great love; and fourth, when I gave up the *Little Review*.

Our talk explored also the psychology of combat. Jane taught me new ways to defend myself, taught me to develop my powers of speech instead of placing myself guilelessly in the enemy's hands, taught me that revenges induce respect. She taught me how to gauge an audience —how to give what was desired or merited but no more— that giving too much was as bad as giving too little. I pounced on this knowledge. I assimilated it. And I have almost never been able to use it.

*   *   *   *   *   *

California was kind to us and we were not particularly kind to it. There had been a certain publicity about our having brought the *Little Review* to the coast for the summer and the first issue to be brought out was awaited with excitement. But, maddened by the interest of our conversations and by the lack of interest in the manuscripts that came in, I decided that I would not contribute to the perpetuation of the uninteresting. The only gesture of protest I could think of was to publish an issue of the magazine made up of sixty-four empty pages, stating that since no art was being produced we would make no attempt to publish any. Jane drew some cartoons of our occupations

124

—Mason and Hamlin, anarchist meetings, horse-back riding, fudge breakfasts and intellectual combats. These filled the two pages in the centre, and all the other pages were reproachfully blank.

We were in fact having the time of our lives. We did a great deal of riding. After a few inglorious horse deals on my part we acquired two animals that lasted out the summer. At first I had a seasoned mare named Maud with a habit of placing her front feet over the edge of precipices. Since she seemed so bored by my lack of stunt riding I decided to trade her in for something less erratic. I went into Mill Valley and found a man willing to sell his horse for five dollars. The horse seemed rather tired on the way back to the ranch so I got off and led it. Jane saw us coming.

What have you got there? she called.

Only cost five dollars, I called back.

Yes, but you'll have the burial costs.

The next morning we put the horse between the shafts of our wagon and pushed it back to town.

Inter your own animals, Jane requested the owner.

Finally, I found a little bucking brown beast and Jane acquired a solid cart horse. After a few harrowing mishaps we became expert cowboys, standing in the stirrups and emitting Indian yells.

*　*　*　*　*　*

I had looked forward to presenting Jane to the anarchists as an incentive toward their clearer thinking. I never dreamed that the pleasure would be almost entirely Jane's.

Berkman and Jane were congenial, but she and Emma Goldman rather less so. During the arguments of our first evening Jane found E.G.'s "geography too vague," her logic non-existent. She teased E.G. and turned to Berkman for sympathy in her laughing comments on the feminine mind.

The next day E.G. told me that she found Jane Heap aggressive.

I felt as if she were pushing me against a wall, she complained.

But I'm twice as violent as Jane, I said.

It doesn't matter. No one can get angry with you. We all know your bark is worse than your bite.

But by the next meeting nearly everybody was angry and chiefly with me. They had tried to maintain that "The Ballad of Reading Gaol" was better art than "Salomé." When I used the black swan in Amy Lowell's "Malmaison" to illustrate a certain way of pointing emotion there was a general uprising. E.G. was a little beside herself.

The working-man hasn't enough leisure to be interested in black swans, she thundered. What's that got to do with the revolution?

But that isn't the argument, I groaned. I walked around the room imprecating the ceiling. Jane had become ominously silent.

We're talking art, not economics, I pointed out. Anyway it makes no difference. Leisure may only give people more time to be insensible.

If only a few people understand the art you talk about that's the proof that it's not for humanity, said Berkman.

Even an oppressed working-man understands the eternal human emotions, I cried. Take the most exquisite of the Imagists—take Ezra Pound's

> The rustling of the silk is discontinued,
> Dust drifts over the courtyard,
> There is no sound of footfall, and the leaves
> Scurry into heaps and lie still,
> And she the rejoicer of the heart is beneath them.
> A wet leaf that clings to the threshold.

That's in the nine eternal moods.

Eternal poppycock! said E.G., behaving like a nervous woman for the first and only time in my experience with her.

At midnight we left to go back to the ranch. I was heartbroken about the black swan. Walking down the San Francisco hills toward the ferry station I had to stop and cry against the buildings. On the ferryboat the moonlight revived me. One of the impressions I have retained of California is that it is always moonlight there. . . .

127

In my disappointment with the anarchists my one resource as usual was to write letters. I began a series of
letter-lectures to Emma Goldman. She had given me a
particularly good occasion in regard to a painter who had
done lifelike portraits of her and Berkman.

He's a great artist, she proclaimed. And so of course
he and his family will starve to death. The world will
recognize him only after he is dead.

I didn't consider him an artist so I sent her some forty
pages of excoriating explanation.

I summarized this and other rebellions in the next number of the L.R. By way of protest Upton Sinclair cancelled
his subscription.

Please cease sending me the *Little Review*, he wrote.
I no longer understand anything in it, so it no longer interests me.

I replied: Please cease sending me your socialist paper.
I understand everything in it, therefore it no longer interests me.

* * * * * *

By early autumn our conversations on the ranch had
attained such proportions that our physical lives had to
be completely readjusted to them. There was such a spell
upon us when our talk went well that it was difficult—it
was destroying—to break it up by saying good-night,
going to bed, and calling out from one room to the other

our final intellectualizations. It seemed to me that this shock could be avoided with a little ingenuity. So I moved our beds (divans) into the living room, placing them on the floor at each side of and at right angles to the fireplace. Between them I put a low table and we dined in pajamas in order to avoid the brutality of breaking up the conversation to undress. There was nothing to do after dinner but push the table away, light another cigarette, and when we could talk no more fall off to sleep under the impression that we hadn't stopped.

Nothing has ever been more delightful than the California rainy season spent in this rather exotic fashion. In the mornings I rode my horse through the dripping forests to the inn at the heart of Muir Woods, filled my knapsack with provisions, and came back to find Jane making biscuits for lunch. Afterward we covered the table with *Little Review* work. I had never found any pleasure in answering the letters that came in, usually accompanied by bad manuscripts. I hid them away like a squirrel in inaccessible places. But Jane adored writing to people. Her first idea in joining the *Little Review* was to be its amanuensis. She spent her time answering letters with exaggerated interest (real) and in planning new typographies which we could never afford. I planned forthcoming issues, especially those filled with articles I meant to extract from Jane. After tea we walked under the misty eucalyptus trees, chiefly for the comfort of returning to the fire-lit room. Then we dressed elaborately in pajamas, discussed sensuous plans for dinner, and pre-

pared it in a kitchen lighted only by a kerosene lamp—
which I absently kept placing on the stove to see what
went on there. . . .

But long before the rainy season I had come upon the
element in Jane's nature with which it was impossible for
me to cope. That is, I can cope with it whenever I find it.
Anyone can. No one should.

I refer to that tendency to live life on the basis of personal conflict—that drama of the compensations—which
to me is entirely devoid of interest. It is so simple to live
without these confusions. Much too simple, says Jane.

For all her intelligence Jane acts upon an ancient instinct that life without dramatics is likely to become
bovine. This was particularly unjust in relation to me. I
am no partisan of the simple life. I adore personal manias.
No relationship could interest me that hadn't a long pen-
dulum of manias, moods, exploited foibles, a thousand
dramatized reserves. These are the conscious dramas—
the charming unrealities that I demand. The unconscious
dramas are the realities that I avoid—the small vulgarities
known as bad humor, the disagreeable answer, the distor-
tion of the impersonal into the personal, those capacities
known as brooding, sulking, pouting, the necessity to assert one's domination, the preoccupation with one's self-
importance, the egoism which conceals its wounds by
being lofty about something else, or expresses its rage by
being incensed about something else. . . . I wish to state

that all these manifestations of the human animal bore me, bore me, *bore* me. Jane hasn't them all—she doesn't need more than one or two of them since she possesses these to such magnitude.

I don't know what poor human being first discovered the fact that the surest way to hold people's interest is to subject them to torment. It is true. But it's so obnoxious a fact that one would be ashamed to act upon one's discovery. If you have an imagination you don't need induced drama. Just once to have realized that the person you love will one day die—and what can you do about it; just once to have understood that you will die and will in all probability have found out nothing either of life or of death—this is enough drama for a lifetime. But people don't reflect on these things. They achieve a great sense of living by living thoroughly those conflicts known as "scenes." Men, even when bored, are flattered under such ministrations. Women are no better. In fact the human race declares that it hates scenes and is in reality enamored of little else.

My freedom from scenes gave Jane no freedom for power. It became irresistible to her to see if I couldn't in some way be drawn into the attraction of the human whirlpool. Her favorite device was the suicide theme. I have nothing against suicide. But indulged in merely as a contemplation and a menace I have always found it slightly repellant. Jane's *leit motif* ran as follows:

The light is too brutal for me here. I am going back to that grave from which I came.

131

The rest of the summer for me was an endurance test in relation to a revolver. I knew that Jane kept it in her studio in a trunk. The trunk was visible from the living room. I wanted Jane to feel I ignored its existence. So I sat in the living room and held myself prepared. I don't know how I stood the strain. But this was in the epoch when I still thought that I had a constitution that could stand anything. I had thought all my life that I must stand everything. I didn't know until years later, when I went to France, that this attitude was American and that I could discard it. This revelation took place among roses, in Normandy, on the terrace of the chateau of Tancarville. . . . It occurred to me that I couldn't, I wouldn't, I wasn't forced to stand anything.

This was in the spring of 1923. I relaxed in A. D. 1923.

*   *   *   *   *   *

The rains continued gently and we knew that we ought to take the *Little Review* back to Chicago. But first we had to take the Mason and Hamlin back to San Francisco. A truck as large as the ranch house and four men, including Axel a Swede, came for it. They placed it easily enough upon the truck though it weighed tons and started off down the mountain roads. Ten minutes later Axel came back alone asking to borrow our ax. What for? Nothing —I haf joost to cut down some trees. We felt that it was perhaps some private enterprise or enthusiasm and gave him the ax. Then we heard great chopping, cutting and falling in the distance and went to see what was going on.

The motor truck stood on a curve in the road with one rear wheel óver the precipice and the others ready to follow. The Mason and Hamlin stood high in the air waiting the slightest touch to fall three hundred feet. Trees were falling all around. The men put them under the truck, hoisted up the piano and careened toward San Francisco.

So did Jane and I.

Mr. Chase told us good-by with tears in his eyes, saying that he loved poetry too.

We stopped in Los Angeles for subscriptions—went on to Denver and collected enough for railroad fare to Chicago.

We had a large revolutionary public in Denver and I shall always remember that city as the place where we gave ourselves seriously to reforming the anarchist mind. (In the natural course of events I had naturally turned from anarchism.)

We argued for three days and nights. Jane met all comers and made nice distinctions for them between feeling and emotion, between fancy and imagination, between good and bad art. I have never known a people more rabid about art than the anarchists. Anything and everything is art for them—that is, anything containing an element of revolt. We tried in vain to divorce them from their exclusive preoccupation with subject matter. But the anarchists like the rest of the world (as I found out later) have a feeling that you mean workmanship only when

133

you talk about style and that by "art" you mean some Flaubertian perfection of "technique." I have never tried to explain the *Little Review's* point of view to anyone—except a few artists—without being accused of didacticism, dogmaticism, fanaticism, æstheticism, exoticism, a debauch of art for art's sake. (I never knew what was wrong with art for art's sake. Should it be art for money's sake? Is there something the matter with art that it dare not exist for itself alone?) It is certain that the *Little Review* has printed work which will not hold up as art. This is inevitable. But I have always accepted or rejected manuscripts on one basis: art as the person. An artist is an exceptional person. Such a person has something exceptional to say. Exceptional matter makes an exceptional manner. This is "style." In an old but expressive phrase, style is the man. But even after stating this sane view clearly enough to be understood by an infant class the argument goes on forever as it did in Denver:

You can't say arbitrarily that this is exceptional and that isn't.

Why not? asked Jane. Art is my business. I wouldn't attempt to tell you that I know more about your business than you do. But you are perfectly willing to treat me in that way.

It's different. There are many opinions about art. No one agrees. Art is something that one judges with the emotions.

Yes, with the art emotions.

Everyone has those emotions.

Not at all. Many people have no emotions beyond the human ones.

You can't say that. It's a statement you can't prove.

No? Only copper wire carries electricity, explained Jane patiently. Other wire doesn't.

Well—(this was always offered as the final unanswerable challenge) all that can be done is the establishment of two autocracies of opinion. You recognize only one.

There never have been two, I fumed.

You can't prove it. Even artists disagree among themselves.

Can't prove it? asked Jane. An airplane is an airplane if it stays up. Otherwise it isn't.

Yes, but who decides what art 'stays up'?

The masters.

But who are the masters? You talk about Leonardo as a master. Who said so? Just because we're in the habit of hearing that—

All right, answered Jane, giving up. I don't know anything about it. Maybe Columbus didn't discover America.

*   *   *   *   *   *

We arrived in Chicago and at once I knew we should go to New York. This was an inconvenient thought. Also an unhappy one for Jane who would never in those days leave any place she loved. Besides I had no reasons to give. It was just "the time to go."

In the interval of convincing Jane there seemed nothing

135

better to do than to take a house and, naturally, furnish it. We rented a floor of three rooms on the North Side, lured by the walls which, under dampness, had acquired the look of Italian frescoes. Then a kind-hearted woman on the South Side offered us a mansion. We switched quickly, lured this time by warmth and comfort and the possibility of giving a Christmas party. Jane would throw away a month any time on a real party—meaning two weeks of decorations, one week of producing presents, one week of preparing food, and extra time somewhere for conceiving the Christmas tree. No conventional tree ever adorned our various houses. Jane made beautiful ones by whitening the branches and hanging them with silver and blue; placing them against a midnight sky of blue cloth with stars, or against gold.

We hung the principal rooms of the new house with white cheescloth to hide the wall paper, and in this glamour brought out an issue of the *Little Review*—during which time I talked about New York. I found my reasons for wanting to go. Chicago had had all it wanted from us, we had had all that it could give. It was time to touch the greatest city of America. It would then be time for Europe. The only way to make the L.R. the international organ I had planned was to publish it from New York where our position would be more commanding. We hadn't yet met all the interesting people in the world. Some of them were in New York. Some were in London and Paris—the greatest artists of the modern age. I loved

Chicago forever, I could never forget it, I would come back to it . . . but I must go on.

* * * * * *

During our last days in Chicago we met someone who has also loved it above other cities—Mary Garden. Jane had written in the current L.R. that Mary made Galli-Curci and other prima donnas look like lost cloak models wandering about the stage.

I sent her a copy of the magazine, telling her we should like to know her, having proselyted for her since the L.R. began. She answered in a swift and beautiful scrawl: Come to-morrow at four.

We went to the Blackstone where she was staying. I was chiefly concerned with the possibility of establishing some real talk with her. Or would she be conventional?

Well, said Jane, she's from the north. I know the people of the north—(Jane is Scandinavian: her mother came from the extremity of Norway that touches Iceland). They know what's what, though they say very little.

She's Scotch, I said. (I am Scotch.) She has the canny Scotch eye. And I think she can be talked to. (It never occurred to me in those days that anyone but Jane would do the talking. It doesn't now.)

We were shown into a salon whose outstanding feature was an enormous photograph of Oscar Wilde on the piano. From an adjoining room a voice of electric vibrations was giving instructions to a waiter, and then Mary pushed open the door and advanced upon us like a battery.

The air was charged with an animal magnetism that one rarely has the pleasure of feeling. Paderewski is devitalized by comparison. The challenge of Mary Garden's presence is one of the most thrilling human experiences I remember. She wore a dark blue suit of a cut that is almost never achieved by any tailor, and a small hat made of pale blue feathers. She sat in a chair like Thais in the mirror scene, hips held back, arms dropping straight.

Where did you get such a body? asked Jane.

I don't know, answered Mary simply. They just gave it to me—("they" meaning the gods, we assumed easily). My sisters haven't it. I don't do anything for it—except tennis—

She sat in her chair surveying her body as if it were a separate entity over which she had a perfect control and in which she could take a complete pride. There was nothing of the prima donna about her. If she hadn't been a singer she would have been a great lawyer, she told us, radiating enough energy to have saved Oscar Wilde from the English.

I carry that photograph with me always, she went on, looking toward the piano. A great poet, a great man. If I had only been where I am to-day, I would have gone to the prison when he came out, taken him with me, re-established him before the world.

There was nothing enveloped, nothing enveloping about Mary Garden's charm. It had none of the suavity of Bernhardt's. It was tangible, unadorned, compelling.

138

What I liked most about her was the quality of her attention.

Let's talk about life, I suggested.

What do you mean? asked Mary, looking frightened.

Oh, I mean abstractly. How do you feel about it?

What she means, said Jane, is that you must find the material a little short.

Mary changed to an armchair. She relaxed in it and began to look more direct than people can look.

Go on, she said.

So Jane went on. She sketched an article she meant to write for the L.R., analyzing Mary's art ideas. Mary Garden furnishes a striking example, in the visual arts, of the artist "creating in his own image."

I am going to begin, said Jane, by saying that the art of the actor to-day is concerned only with the reproduction of the few galvanized words and actions of mankind. This attests nothing but a lack of consciousness, lack of movement, lack of ecstasy. As I see it, you alone on the stage are theatric. You summarize, enforce the design, create a new aspect, indicate the infinite from the concrete—by form and movement.

Mary listened intently. She sat deeper in her chair, her head forward and down, her eyes boring up under the eyelids.

Yes, she said when Jane had finished.

*   *   *   *   *   *

We prepared to say farewell to Chicago. Jane spent the

days in a coma of regret and indecision. I felt the only demand I would make of life henceforth would be to know
people whose inclination was not to "turn aside and
brood."

We went to the offices of *Poetry* to say good-by to Harriet Monroe and found Glenway Westcott beginning his
career there. He was reviewing a book of ridiculous poetry
by Michael Strange, and his comments were pertinent.
Glenway had such clipped and distinguished speech that I
thought he was English. No, he explained, he came from
Wisconsin but he loved the English language and had
trained himself to speak it beautifully. He hadn't yet done
anything he could offer to the L.R. I shall always regret
not having published his work for I like it as well as anything that has come out of America—with the exception
of Hemingway's. I don't know just how it happened that
we heard nothing more of him until "The Apple of the
Eye" which was published after I had left New York for
Paris and the *Little Review* had become an annual rather
than a quarterly. It was in Paris that I was able to tell Glenway how much I liked his novels.

I'm an old-fashioned writer, don't you think?

Not at all. Or only in the sense that you have more
accretions than are fashionable.

By accretions I meant those strata of personal experience
which some people manage to acquire out of little and
others fail to acquire out of much. In "Grandmothers"
Glenway Westcott shows by his precise objective imagination more knowledge of himself than one can find in any

current American fiction that I know of. He has made his past his own—a far more exciting performance for instance than Sherwood Anderson's continued subjectivity which leaves him in the state of vague romanticism about himself that he undoubtedly enjoyed at the age of ten.

I told everyone good-by—including the Fine Arts Building. I went to walk through its corridors which always seemed to me filled with flowers—its shops, which gave me the emotion of a perpetual Christmas. I talked for the last time with the elevator boys, the head starter, the night watchman. They assured me that the Fine Arts wouldn't be the same without me, that Chicago wouldn't be the same. I went to buy a rose from the flower woman around the corner, where my single rose purchases at five cents had left a great tenderness.

Jane and I wandered in the streets at night. Once when it was snowing we went to the North Side and walked around the block where her gold room still existed in a house that had been sold to insensible people.

Last of all I went to a symphony concert. Coming back to the Fine Arts Building I met Ben Hecht.

After you have gone, he announced, I'm going to have an electric sign put across this building:

Where is Athens now?

NEW YORK

The exodus to New York had been planned minutely, except in its financial aspects. Fortunately at the eleventh hour Lawrence Langner came to town and heard of the project.

I'm being paid seventy-five dollars for a play *Vanity Fair* is publishing this month. Let me present it for the New York trip.

It has always pleased me to remember that *Vanity Fair* paid our way to New York. This magazine had persistently ignored our existence; refused later to speak of James Joyce and "Ulysses" in the pioneer days when such action would have helped; and, when it commissioned Sherwood Anderson to conduct a sporting page, coldly turned down his suggestion to make his first article a tribute to the sporting quality of my *Little Review* venture.

The Christmas party was such a success that Jane boarded the train in an afterglow of happiness. The first few hours out of Chicago passed in talking of how charming the tree had been, the gifts, the fête. We have spent a large part of our lives talking of how happy we were going to be, were being, had been. . . . But the reality of New York soon began to make itself felt and I noticed that Jane took from her pocket a little box of sachet and held it in her hand. It was the sachet of the gold room. I tried not to see. Jane tried to be gay, but she kept looking surreptitiously at the box and smelling it until we had to succumb frankly to the fact that everything was going to be pretty bad.

When we pulled into New York we went from bad to worse. Jane wouldn't look out of the taxi window. I fought back the hideous reality of such an arrival. I tried to enter the city on a charger.

We went directly to the Brevoort Hotel. My plan was to take a bus up Fifth Avenue and Riverside Drive. But Jane had other plans. She threw herself face down on her bed and stayed there.

What can I do?

Silence.

But let me do something. It's too sad like this.

Let me alone.

So I went out on a bus alone and struggled again with reality.

When I came back to the Brevoort Jane was in the same position on the bed. She stayed there without moving until morning. I sat in a chair all night and wondered where my beautiful triumphant life was. I began to be afraid I couldn't achieve it.

One of the most difficult experiences of life for me is the endurance of another's suffering. I should much rather suffer myself. I've a fixation, an inheritance, against un-happiness. And in Jane's case there was a second cause which made her unhappiness insupportable to me. I had learned that there is an abstract grief that matters, as dis-tinguished from a typical grief that doesn't. Some tears count, others don't. Jane never cried just tears.

My heart is an Idiot, Jane once wrote. I write my name and way and pin it on him . . . if we should become separated. With my hands I take my brain and slowly uncrumple it. I smooth out every crease and wrinkle. There is nothing to press it out upon except abysses. It is a long job and wearing—sur-prising how big it is smoothed out like melted silk. I will crumple it up again firmly and put it back after I have left it this way for a long time shining and clean. The years breed pain when one is accomplice with an Idiot.

The burden of Jane's unhappiness was an integral part of her genius. I wanted that genius for the *Little Review*. I had seen no more highly organized mental-emotional equipment anywhere. I had chosen her mind as represen-tative of what I called the creative mind. I wanted the *Little Review* to reflect this point of view above any other. The Clive Bell mind, Benvenuto Croce and others of that type were merely "æsthetic." Jane had the mind of a maker. By infinite persuasion I could prevail upon her to translate herself into terms for public consumption. But why force anyone to do anything? Especially something she didn't want to do. The hopelessness of our situation sometimes appalled me. Perhaps we should separate our lives. We were on different curves—one going, one coming. Jane should be allowed to stay on in Chicago, though I knew where that would lead her—to years of giving out priceless talk to friends or relatives who would never retain a word of it. Without the right audience she would never exploit her unique gifts. I was her best audience: I could goad her into talking. But could I stay girded up to this necessity? Why not? Who has ever found that one extra necessity—or a dozen for that matter—could stop a life?

By morning I was dauntless again.

*　　*　　*　　*　　*　　*

I don't remember what we went through during the next ten days. I made a conscious effort to forget it. Certainly it wasn't like a beginning in New York. It was like an ending in the tomb.

Finally, we found a studio at 31 West Fourteenth Street, in the old Van Buren house. It was in the basement, in what had evidently been the kitchens. It cost twenty-five dollars a month. There was a fair-sized square room for the office and back of it a smaller room giving on to a stone porch from which one mounted steps into a "garden." Something like plans began for us again.

We gave our minds first to the pressing financial problems that beset us. I regret not being able to recall in detail how we dealt with these tragedies. I couldn't both remem-

145

ber and survive, and to survive I was determined. From this time (1917) until 1923 there was almost never a week when the morning coffee was assured. As the *Little Review* became more articulate, more interesting, its subscription list became less impressive. It is much easier to find a public for ideals than for ideas. The subscriptions dwindled during the whole of the L.R.'s best period. We tried every other way of keeping it alive. Jane often said we survived only because I looked as if we had money; because whatever the strain I continued to feel that we had.

My most vivid memory of the first days in New York is of one night in the Brevoort when Jane, who appeared to have reached despair, decided to write her article on Mary Garden. I didn't attempt to probe the causes of this mysterious conjunction but prepared to listen, encourage and note. For one week we scarcely went out. We walked about a room and talked; sat silent and thought; ate delicatessen food and discussed—my contribution being to convince Jane that anything one could formulate in words could be transcribed to paper without losing in the transition. I had always said that Jane's writing for the L.R. was a matter of life or death for me. I meant it. During the week my great friend, the czarina with the ailing heart, passed through New York for two days. I went to see her with misgivings about the article. From her hotel I telephoned to Jane.

How is the article going?

Not at all, answered Jane in a dying tone.

I flew back to the Brevoort. We talked all night. The

next morning the doctors had prescribed an early departure for Chicago and a few weeks later, before I could see her again, the czarina died.

Excerpts from Jane's article:

. . . In all the arts, whenever the magic of the artist has been united with this other magic (personality) the possessor has been of the first great . . . I wonder why, even in those people to whom has come some appreciation of the magic of the artist, there is still so often such strong resentment and distrust of this other magic. Because of their adventures in the great emotions those who have it loosen new forces of life; they re-create the great passions; they add something to Fate.

Everyone feels that he has a right to a share in that which the millions are working together in uproar to add to existence. Many long for a share in that which the artists are making in silence for the soul. But who is there except the artist who is willing to feel in this thing the imminence of something beyond life and personality? Who else in the world except the lonely insane, because of their adventures in illusions and hallucinations, ever add anything to Fate? How easy to say that genius is akin to madness. All great antitheses are akin: all unknown things are mysteriously akin, as all known things are naturally akin. But how poignantly akin are the known and unknown.

. . . When I was a little child I lived in a great asylum for the insane. It was a world outside of the world, where realities had to be imagined and where, even through those excursions in illusions and hallucinations, there ran a strange loneliness. The world can never be so lonely in those places where the mind has never come as in a place where the mind has gone. . . . There was no one to ask about anything. There was no way to make a connection with "life". . . . Very early I had given up everyone except the Insane. The others knew nothing about anything, or knew only uninteresting facts. From the Insane I could get everything. They knew everything about nothing and were my authority; but beyond that there was a silence. Who had made the pictures, the books and the music in the world? And how had they made them? And how could you tell the makers from just people? Did they have a light around their heads? Were there any of them in the world now? And would I ever see one? . . . Then a name came across the world, with a new radiance— Mary Garden.

Mary Garden seems to be the only singer who knows that all the arts come from the same source and follow the same laws. . . . None of the arts expresses human emotion—they express the *source* of human emotion. To express the emotion of life is to live; to express the life of emotion is to make art. . . . I wish I could tell what a great creative artist Mary Garden is. It is one thing for the artist to create a character within the outlines definitely or indefinitely drawn by the composer; to put himself in the place of the character and act as he would act. But the creative artist *takes the character to himself* and then creates from his imagination in his own image. The more universal the artist the greater his power to reveal his soul in different images. . . .

Mary Garden is a great decorative actress. I am using decoration in the sense in which it is used in painting, where elimination and not elaboration is used to emphasize the intention of line and color . . . She can draw in the whole psychology of a scene with one line of her body—the line of her walk. If she is to dominate a situation with her intellect or her beauty she walks from the centre of her intelligence, which is the head; if it is a matter of the soul she walks from the centre of her presence, which is the top plane of the chest . . . This is living painting which moves in rhythm like a frieze.

148

The famous Mabel Dodge soirées had ceased to be before my arrival on the New York scene. The first glorious days of Greenwich Village were over. Polly's on Fourth Street had given way to Christine's on MacDougall Street, over the newly-opened Provincetown Theatre, which soon began offering one-act plays of Eugene O'Neill. Max Eastman was editing the *Masses* and writing books on the appreciation of poetry.

I had known Max Eastman for some time. He seemed to me to lack the fire I wanted to associate with him and his ideas. This was partly due to the fact that he was a socialist. I could never listen to the socialists. Anarchism, like all great things, is an announcement. Your "magnetic centre" can do what it likes with that. Socialism is an explanation and falls, consequently, into the realm of secondary things.

One of my first evenings in New York was spent in Edna Kenton's book-lined apartment in West Fifteenth Street with Ida Rauh, Fania Marinoff, Helen Westley, Phillip Moeller, and Carl Van Vechten. Intellectually I considered it a singularly second-rate evening. I found the same difference between the quality of the talk in Chicago and New York (in Chicago's favor) that I found later between that of New York and Paris (in New York's favor). I shall never forget the first month I spent in Paris. I thought I should expire of the general slowing-up of all processes (mental, emotional, physical). Everyone seemed so toned down that any display of mental or emotional vitality became brutal—something like visiting your grandmother. You feel too dazzling for the situation.

In Chicago there had been a fresher more passionate interest than I could find in New York. At Edna Kenton's they all seemed to be exchanging book information rather than personal points of view. I finally became too irritated to control myself and forthwith offered a display of my porcupine nature which so perfectly conceals my intelligence that people wonder why on earth Jane Heap ever took *me* on the staff of the *Little Review!*

The conversation had turned upon pianists. I tried to inject a little flavor into its commonplaceness by talking of Harold Bauer as an exponent of modern piano methods. I felt that this might lead into those regions of precise psychological thinking that are my delight. But not at all. Everybody insisted that Bauer didn't take you off your feet with emotion, or send hot (or cold) shivers up (or down) your spine. Finding the intellectuals of New York still lingering in these primer realms was too much for me. At some particularly vacuous remark of Carl Van Vechten's I turned upon him.

My word, I cried with scorn, don't you know anything at all about music?

This was considered superfluous by everyone present, inasmuch as Carl was rated (with "Music and Bad Manners" and other early work) as one of New York's expert writers on music with an unlimited fund of musical knowledge. A fund of anecdotes, I call that kind of thing —intellectual gossip, echoes of information, a cataloging of current impressions, a snobbery of opinion. I disapprove of snobbery in matters of thought as intensely as I approve of it in matters of dress. Good thinking never springs from snobbery—good dressing from little else.

Everyone was disgusted with me that evening. Even Jane wouldn't rescue the soirée from disaster.

Your technique is too infantile, she complained later.

I decided to become mature. I would be calm, careful, contained. I would proceed henceforth by the time-honored methods of exposition and comparison, of reason and logic. I decided this, and gave up after the first attempt. This reasonable and convincing procedure gave me no emotional recompense. And since my object in talking is neither to learn nor to convey but to enter into new emotional states, since I can't produce ideas unless they are forced out of me by an emotional explosion, I have gone on all my life being infantile. It was only quite lately that I imposed upon myself for the first time, successfully, the winning of a new type of emotional reward. I began an argument with a clear conception of what I meant to say, led my antagonist into saying the things necessary to illustrate my point, calculated carefully the moment when his feeling would get the better of his mind, helped him to commit this blunder which I have committed with such consummate ease all my life, and in the end extracted a certain pleasure from the game rather than exclusively from the matter of the discussion. I shall try this again one day. It is rather pathetic to reflect that it has taken me thirty years to create a new experience for myself—that the operation of a temperament ("agitation in the void") should have robbed half my life of the profit of new functionings.

*   *   *   *   *   *

For living quarters we found a floor at 24 West Sixteenth Street, in a house that had once been the residence of William Cullen Bryant. This in some way endeared it to us. After all, Bryant wasn't Longfellow.

There were four rooms, the two large living rooms being of exquisite proportions. I loved the old New York houses. We soon discovered that ours had an undertaking business on the ground floor and an exterminator company in the basement. But did it matter?

After the usual piano arrangements had been made we concentrated all our efforts on Jane's room. It was to be a room where all *Little Review* conversation would take place. It was to be a special, haunting, poignant, dedicated room. It was. In this room the *Little Review* entered into its creative period.

We decorated it ourselves. It took several months—first to find the money, then the time. We bought gold Chinese paper at a Japanese paper shop, in long oblong strips. Papering the walls with these required Chinese patience, as they were disposed to tear under the most delicate touch. The woodwork was pale cream, the floor dark plum, the furniture old mahogany. The feature of the room was a large divan hung from the ceiling by heavy black chains. It was covered with a dull-toned blue and on it were four silk cushions—emerald green, magenta, royal purple, tilleul. Between the windows was a large reading table with a lemon yellow lamp.

Here the poets, writers, painters came to see us, seeking an entry into the *Little Review*. Jane loves human contacts. On the contrary people devitalize me, so it was usually Jane who received them. She retained their manuscripts, saying that I would examine, accept or reject them. But somehow they always felt that the rejections came from her. Appearances are deceitful. Jane looked solid and redoubtable, I looked easily influenced. They wanted to deal with me.

Certainly you can see her, Jane told Alfred Kreymborg, laughing. She's kinder than I am but less hopeful.

The younger poets came for talk. We had long discussions on the making of poetry—stamping it indelibly with the element of one's self, measuring the area of one's personal existence, searching the specific gravity of emotions, weighing the content of one's thought, checking up on one's observation.

Hart Crane came in with one of his first poems. It contained a vague reference to the immaculate white ice of Norway.

Immaculate is a dirty word to use, said Jane. That ice is so white it looks black.

One night at Lola Ridge's, in a group of future poets, the polemic seemed so inferior to our gold-room flights that I began prodding Jane to perform. Tired of being treated like a trained bear Jane became intensely Norwegian and for once told the public some of the things she thought. Emmanuel Carnevalli and Louis Grudin, two young poets of promise, became so angry that they left. The next day they came to find Jane in Sixteenth Street.

We hated you so much that we went out and walked all night, they confessed. You left no hope for anyone. But now we want to hear more.

Sometimes people of no talent came and begged us to help them. I remember one young girl with gaunt eyes and the earnestness that would prevent anyone from achieving anything. She was writing stories about the miseries of miners and other tragedies of mankind in which she had never participated.

What shall I do to become a good writer?

First disabuse yourself of the national idea that genius is a capacity for hard work, I suggested. The meaning of genius is that it doesn't have to work to attain what people without it must labor for—and not attain.

Yes, but what shall I do?

Use a little lip rouge, to begin with. Beauty may bring you experiences to write about.

Sometimes opposing factions gathered in the gold room for debate. Their attitude toward us and our ideas were invariably in the beginning antagonistic. We were considered heartless, flippant, ruthless, devastating. But we never found a really exciting resistance. After an hour or two we would stand revealed as two simple sincere people with serious ideas. "Sincerity" was the great test in those days. Because we could always laugh we were always suspected of being frivolous.

I have never been able to understand the overwhelming interest in sincerity, Jane would say. Do you ask a woman if she is sincere when she sews?

The debates usually ended in Jane's talking for both sides.

Oh come on, she urged the silent audience. A good answer deserves a good question.

To me the most interesting of all these discussions was speculation of a type that is not the property of the savant mind (at least has not been in our time)—speculation as to what produces permanence of emotion; the transcription of feeling into that state which becomes known as emotion (Knut Hamsun: "the moon, a white scale in the sky"); by what touch does one immortalize objects? by what power does one create in one's own image; what is the criterion of an image by which to create? what is the poignant human being? by what signs is he known? what is the distinction between sensibility and sensitization?— the explanation of their curious lack in organisms often sensitively nervous or delicately trembling but utterly unsensitized?

Jane and I spent our lives over these matters. We were a great disappointment to the *literati*. Somehow we could never lead the kind of life that appeared normal for them. They could never count on finding us day after day in the

restaurants or other haunts of the intellectually gregari-
ous. We seemed to bear little relation to the younger generation bent on escaping the home. No sooner had we escaped than we began to create a hearthstone. We were
dedicated to the ceremonies of living. We insisted upon
living beautifully. And since we hadn't a penny we had to
produce this condition for ourselves. It took the best part
of our youth and energy. We kept our house in the most
perfect order. We cleaned, scrubbed, dusted, cooked,
washed dishes. We made our own fires, cleaned our
hearths—we could never afford a charwoman. We did
our own shopping—chose our own meats and vegetables
—and as Jane had an intelligent old-fashioned prejudice
against canned foods, hulled our own peas. We washed
and ironed our own clothes. We cut our own hair—very
well, too. And Jane made a suit of such perfect architec-
ture that when I showed it later to one of New York's
leading tailors he remarked:

This suit is beautifully cut and made. May I ask who
did it?

It was made by a painter.

Impossible.

Well, by a writer.

You're joking. Still if I had to choose between the two
I'd say a painter. No writer could do it.

We did everything, it seemed to me, but produce our
own stockings and shoes. I'm rather ashamed the idea of
making stockings didn't occur to me. Jane would have
been equal to it, I'm sure.

Besides this domesticity we brought out the *Little Review* every month—almost literally brought it out ourselves. We hired the cheapest printer in New York, Mr. Popovitch, whose mother had been poet laureate of Serbia. He had two daughters. They all took a personal interest in the magazine. We went to their shop in East Twenty-third Street and helped with the setting-up, to gain time—and lost much time helping the daughters to read Wyndham Lewis. On Sundays to push things along we often took our lunch and spent the whole day in the print shop, correcting proof, setting type, even folding pages for the binder. It was a good life except when the United States Post Office decided to suppress and burn the magazine. After our heart-breaking labors it was an affront to learn that the four thousand copies had been placed on a (what kind of funeral pyre do they place them on?) and burned to a crisp, all because Wyndham Lewis had written about a man and a girl falling in love.

Summer came—our first summer in New York. It was the hottest New York had had in several seasons. Jane's gold room was finished but so were we. We now had an enchanting place to live in and nothing to live on. It was one of the periods when money absolutely abstained from coming in. Our provisions were also finished. There remained only a sack of potatoes. For three days we ate nothing but potatoes, arranged in every possible way to which the potato will lend itself. Household responsibilities lightened. For a week I had time to play the piano.

A bookbinder (Czechoslovakian) came to see us in the gold room. He had become so interested reading the *Little Review* that he wanted to see what kind of people were publishing it. When he saw he became paternal and begged us to leave off.

You can't carry on such a struggle, he cried violently. It will break you. Stop before it's too late. I've seen the young radicals doing the same thing in the old country. All old before their time. The forces are all against you. They'll kill you.

*   *   *   *   *   *

In 1913-1914 Ezra Pound had issued the first *Blast* manifestos from London. Shortly after the *Little Review* was launched he brought out the first number of *Blast*.

I had corresponded with Ezra since that time but I had never seen him. When he wrote suggesting that the *Little Review* employ his talents as foreign editor we hailed the occasion.

One of the first manuscripts to arrive through his instigation—something I liked as well as anything the *Little Review* ever published—was T. S. Eliot's "Eeldrop and Appleplex" series. Wyndham Lewis sent regularly his best work, through the Tarr period. John Rodker was just beginning to write and Ezra sent us his first poems and critical essays. Another charming series came from Ford Madox Ford (né Hueffer), called "Men and Women." Ezra sent much of his own best writing. His letters alone would have made a good magazine:

Dear M. C. A.,

The Little Review is perhaps temperamentally closer to what I want done???????

DEFINITELY then:

I want an "official organ" (vile phrase). I mean I want a place where I and T. S. Eliot can appear once a month (or once an "issue") and where Joyce can appear when he likes, and where Wyndham Lewis can appear if he comes back from the war.

DEFINITELY a place for our regular appearance and where our friends and readers (what few of 'em there are), can look with assurance of finding us.

I don't know quite how much your pages carry. I don't want to swamp you.

I must have a steady place for my best stuff (apart from original poetry, which must go to "Poetry" unless my guarantor is to double his offer. Even so I oughtn't to desert "Poetry" merely because of convenience.

(I have only three quarrels with them: Their idiotic fuss over christianizing all poems they print, their concessions to local pudibundery, and that infamous remark of Whitman's about poets needing an audience).

As to policy, I don't think I am particularly propagandist. I have issued a few statements of fact, labelled two schools and there has been a lot of jaw about 'em. But an examination of files will show that I have done very little preachy writing.

A monthly should keep some tab on the few interesting books that DO appear in London and Paris.

I should count on Eliot a good deal for such current criticism and appreciation. He is in touch with various papers here and sees what is going on.

I don't know how much Joyce would send in. He is working on another novel.

Lewis is not to be counted on, NOW, by the grace of God he may come back in due season.

The young stuff here that hasn't a home would be an occasional poem from Rodker or Iris Barry and the unknown.

The rest are clustered to the Egoist. I got Aldington that job several years ago. He hasn't done quite as well as I expected, BUT he was very young. H. D. is all right, but shouldn't write criticism.

The Lawrence-Lowell-Flint-Cournos contingent give me no active pleasure. Fletcher is all right now and again, but too diffuse in the intervals.

You advertise "new Hellenism." It's all right if you mean humanism, Pico's "De Dignitate," the Odyssey, the Moscophorous.

Not so good if you mean Alexandria, and worse if you mean the Munich-sham-Greek "Hellas" with a good swabian brogue.

Confucianism is not propagandist, and polytheism would only be misunderstood, so I shant offer any or much competition on these lines. (Perhaps an essay on Confucius? on approval.)

This to be printed straight off. (Bar of course libel, and the usual thing, or the printers refusing ABSOLUTELY to set it up, because of its inflammability.)

If there happens to be more copy the excess would be submitted to you as any other contribution. No hard feelings if you chuck it.

I think we might criticize each other's selections in confidence with SOME freedom and directness? ? ? ?

(as you like . . . it is sometimes amusing . . . I don't insist . . .)

Miss A. "Mr. P. you will annihilate ALL our subscribers."

Mr. P. "Sorry. Your dear Powys is a wind-bag lacking both
balance and ballast."

Miss A. "DO wind-bags have ballast!!!"

Dear M. C. A.,

I enclose another lost sheep. It has taken me months to recover it, samee Fenollosa.

It is not wildly exciting, and it is not news, but it is a small
scrap of Voltaire's Dictionaire Philosophique, which considering its date might serve to show how far far far etc., how long
long long etc., it takes for a light to travel across the darkness of
Anglo-American literature.

I know it is too long, BUT it simply won't cut, and P. 17 with
passage about Sarah is almost worth waiting for.

Also P. 3. "It seems probable that God was not attempting to
educate the jews in philosophy or cosmogony."

Etc. etc. The damned thing has bits, and they wont come out
of the whole mass of it.

Fraser has of course done the whole job monumentally, BUT
good god how slowly, in how many volumes. No reader of the
Golden Bough is likely to relapse into bigotry, but it takes such a
constitution to read it.

A reminder that "There once was a man called Voltaire" can
do no harm. The measure in which he is unread, can I think be
found by printing the fragment as "translated from an eight-
eenth century author" and see how many people place it.

Poetry has just come with a very asinine note on the Feb.
number.

Bad poetry being alike everywhere it is natural that Rimbaud should differ from Longfellow and Vaughn Moody, and Hen Van Dyke, and that Byron from Musset (both romantic and careless writers of same degree of relative goodness and badness) should be about even. Byron rather more snap, a good satirist and a loose writer.

Dear Margaret,

What the ensanguined lllllllllllllll is the matter with this BLOODY goddamndamnblastedbastardbitchbornsonofaputrid-seahorse of a foetid and stinkerous printer ???????

Is his serbo-croatian optic utterly impervious to the twelfth letter of the alphabet????

JHEEZUSMARIAJOSE!!! Madre de dios y de dios del perro. Sacrobosco di Satanas.

OF COURSE IF IF IF bloodywell IF this blasted numero appears with anything like one twohundredandfiftieth part of these errors we are DONE, and I shall never be able to cross the channel or look a French ecrivain in the face. . . .

Dear editor,

The one use of a man's knowing the classics is to prevent him from imitating the false classics.

You read Catullus to prevent yourself from being poisoned by the lies of pundits; you read Propertius to purge yourself of the greasy sediments of lecture courses on "American Literature," on "English Literature from Dryden to Addison"; you (in extreme cases) read Arnaut Daniel so as not to be overawed by a local editor who faces you with a condemnation in the phrase "paucity of rhyme."

The classics "ancient and modern," are precisely the acids to gnaw through the thongs and bulls-hides with which we are tied by our schoolmasters.

162

They are the antiseptics. They are almost the only antiseptics against the contagious imbecility of mankind.

I can conceive an intelligence strong enough to exist without them, but I can not recall having met an incarnation of such intelligence. Some does better and some does worse.

The strength of Picasso is largely in his having chewed through and chewed up a great mass of classicism; which, for example, the lesser cubists, and the flabby cubists have not.

Dear M. C. A.,

He "happens to know" I omitted a name because of personal dislike.

He is a bloody and louse-eaten liar.

As a guide to tender feet, I suggest that my "personal dislike" of individual contemporaries has largely arisen from two causes (also that it has arisen subjectively in the mind or boozum *of the disliked* and not in my own).

Cause 1. a. My unwillingness to praise what seems to me unworthy of praise.

b. My unwillingness, after haing discerned a faint gleam of virtue in a young man's work, or even got some of his stuff printed, then to be unable to note signs of progress in later work, or even to be unable to retain my interest.

Cause 2. My interest (sudden or gradual) in the work of some other artist or writer.

I think there is one slip in the number. "Help us to make the L. R. a power." Bad wording. Nothing but our own blasted contents will do that. Henley was a power, I have heard tell, with the National Observer when its circulation had shrunk to 80 subscribers. I don't want to pursue dominion to that extent, but it is a glorious precedent.

As for my "personal dislikes" of poets. CRRRRHist

JHEEZUS when I think of the hours boredom I have put up with from people MERELY because they have in an unguarded and irrecoverable and irresponsible moment committed a good poem, or several!!!!!!!!!! Ah, that one might live to see the expression on the face of a new poet, whom I had just been boosting, upon seeing another still newer poet seated in an armchair.

And then there is Amy. Is there any life into which the personal Amy would not bring rays of sunshine? Alas! and alas only, that the price, i.e., equal suffrage in a republic of poesy, a recognition of artistic equality, should come between us.

I think, despite the difficulty of knowing what one will think in a year's time, I think, credo che credessi, etc., that dear Amy Lowell's talents and temperament will always be political rather than literary or artistic. She is delightful. ONLY she wanted me to sell out lock stock and barrel, and I said it didn't interest me. And still she would have it, so I named a price, i. e., I said I would contribute to a democratized anthology IF she would institute a yearly prize for poetry to be adjudged by Yeats, Hueffer, and myself. (I even went so far as to name a committee including herself. I can't remember whether it was she, I and Yeats, or she, I and Hueffer, or all four.) But that touched the sacred springs of wrath.

I think she was a bloody fool, for we could have bust the British academic committee (called the British Academy) to smithereens, and she could have been somebody over here (which she wanted to be) rather than being driven back to the Hylo kennels.

Dear M. C. A.,

If London and particularly Mayfair, is going to take up the magazine, we must be more careful than ever NOT to have in too much Amy, and suburbs.

Re / Amy I don't want to hedge too much. I don't think we need bar her from the magazine, but she cant write for the mondaine London clientele. At least I cant see Lady Randolph Churchill (or May Sinclair for example) reading her with any spirit of reverence. These people can take it just as strong as Lewis can pitch. Your own tone suits 'em O. K. (NOT that you'd care a damn if it didn't but you may as well know it.)

Hecht is an asset. Hard reading and a bit heavy, but he has the root of the matter in him. He is trying to come to grips also. When he recalls the fact that Maupassant does not exaggerate, he can write contes—i. e., can (future) will be able to.

Dear Margaret,

Right you are. Re / Quinn, remember: Tis he who hath bought the pictures; tis he who both getteth me an American publisher and smacketh the same with rods; tis he who sendeth me the Spondos Oligos, which is by interpretation the small tribute or spondooliks wherewith I do pay my contributors, WHEREFORE is my heart softened toward the said J. Q., and he in mine eyes can commit nothing heinous.

Can you, on the other hand see Mencken, he writes hoping the suppression wont drive you out of business; and if he chose to wail in his back pages re/ Cantleman (Lewis), it might do some good. After all he still has a circulation. AND his eyes discerned me years since.

Re / Amy. I DONT want her. But if she can be made to liquidate, to excoriate, to cash in, on a magazine, ESPECIALLY in a section over which I have no control, and for which I am not responsible. THEN would I be right glad to see her milked of her money, mashed into moonshine, at mercy of monitors. Especially as appearance in U.S. section does NOT commit me to any approval of her work.

Of course IF (which is unlikely) she ever wanted to return to the true church, and live like an honest woman. Something might be arranged. BUT . . .

Is she yet weary of Braithewaite, and the mulattoism, mental and physical?

Do, or perhaps DO NOT, regard the prospectus of Contemporary Verse. Of all the crapule that a reputed millionaire was ever responsible for . . . I hope it COSTS Storke something.

(Also remember that I CANT possibly know from this side which of my damned suggestions are any good. Probably ANY suggestion I make re/ American policy is bad. However I may as well send 'em. You can reject 'em with perfect ease.)

Etc. I do have to stop and earn my board now and again. Malheureusement.

Dear M. C. A.,

Bodenheim has been on the grump ever since I was forced to tell him that I could not perceive much originality in his work. Neither is there. He was commendable in the first place because he was trying to take more care of his actual wording than either Masters or Sandburg. In verse having no very marked or seductive cadence, no rhyme, no quantitative measure, the actual language must be fairly near to perfection.

Also the foul Bodenheim distorts my words. I said nothing against these poets save that they hadn't opened up anything new during the past three years. Which, damn it, they haven't. I set my period at three years (definitely and deliberately). Thus H. D.'s early work, Aldington's, and William's "Postlude" do not come up for comparison.

I don't think any of these people have gone on; have invented much since the first "Des Imagistes" anthology. H. D. has done work as good. She has also (under I suppose the flow-contamination of Amy and Fletcher) let loose dilutations and

166

repetitions, so that she has spoiled the "few but perfect" position which she might have held on to.

Anyhow Eliot has thought of things I had not thought of, and I'm damned if many of the others have done so. Inventive, creative, or what not.

And the DIAL, OH *gosh,* slosh, tosh, the dial, d, i, a, l, dial. Dial=the stationary part of a clock or other chronometer. AND the "new republic," dessicated, stodgied copy of the dessicated New Statesman. WHY "new," why this passion for "newness" always confined to the title. Put there presumably to keep it out of the way. Not that one desires newness so awfully AWFULLY, goodness would suffice.

Dear Margaret,

Jan. number arrived. Feeling better. Number looks business-like, and "about to continue." Damn, damn, DAMN I must pull myself together and DO something.

I wish to Christ you would take an anaesthetic and print this cursed thing of Kearys; thereby saving me time to breathe and get something written.

Bill Wms. is *the* most bloody inarticulate animal that ever gargled. BUT its better than Amy's bloody ten-cent repetitive gramaphone, perfectly articulate (i. e., in the verbal section).

Whereas the bleating genius of the HOME product. Hecht might write good DeMaupassant if he didn't try to crack jokes and ring bells; and if he would only realize that he DONT need to exaggerate to be interesting.

SANGRE DI SAN PIETRO!!! WHY!!! do you recall that better to be forgotten libellule of Wilkinson's????? Raoul Root INDEED. KHRRIST. Am I a pet pug to have blue ribbons curled in my tail?

Despite your wail Lewis' description of the three American

rescuers in the second half of "Sol. Humour" is excellent, Digit of the Moon, etc. Oh very good. I got him to rewrite some of it, but wot the hell can a man do in his present circumstances. It is, as he recognizes, a question of doing his stories somehow or other, or not doing them at all.

He will, if he dont get killed, revise later before book publication.

Dast it the James and DeGourmet numbers are six months work each. AND I do not want to sink wholly into criticism to the utter stoppage of creation. ETC.

Dear M. C. A.,

Do give me credit occasionally for at least a reason for my acts. Even if it isn't the sole and surviving reason left on the planet; and even if I occasionally do not hit a bull's-eye.

And do for god's sake realize that having graciously wasted a week explaining that I would accept K but could not pay for him; I cannot waste another saying that we will not print him. I have only a certain amount of energy; and that I have (*a*) to get my poetry written; (*b*) to pay my rent etc.; (*c*) assist in the promulgation of the L. R. (Letters to be placed in any order you like.)

There appears to be nothing in America between professors and Krembourgs and Bodenheims. Platonic hemiandroi. Anemia of guts on one side and anemia of education on the other.

As yet since May of last year America has coughed up no "creative" stuff, i.e., no poetry or fiction to the L.R., apart from jh on females with faces with noses level with ears which wasnt fiction. But apart from the editorial the U. S. has given nothing to contents of L. R. save that treacle about Judas which affected me much more violently than K seems to have affected you.

Even so I think you were "right" to print it, on the principle that one must accept *something* now and again, if one is not utterly to choke off all inflow of mss. (a very damned dangerous principle, but pragmatic). And, as you say, I am ageing rapidly. Byron is described as very old, or at least gray and showing age at 36. I have but a few years left me. I cannot be expected to keep up sufficient interest in the state of public imbecility to go on being "astringent" perpetually.

I wonder at what point a discussion of music would lead you and me into mutual assassination??????? Gawd only knows.

Joyce, by the way, approves of the clavichord. And he has also sung in opera. Lewis, I think, regards the instrument as a strange unaccountable sort of mouse-trap; the charwoman (after four months' services) spoke of it the other day as "the little black table" (observation the leading characteristic of the "lower orders").

Chère amie, I am, for the time being, bored to death with being any kind of an editor. I desire to go on with my long poem; and like the Duke of Chang, I desire to hear the music of a lost dynasty. (Have managed to hear it, in fact.) And I desire also to resurrect the art of the lyric, I mean words to be sung, for Yeats' only wail and submit to keening and cha*u*nting (with a *u*) and Swinburne's only rhapsodistify. And with a few exceptions (a few in Browning) there is scarcely anything since the time of Waller and Campion. AND a mere imitation of them wont do.

Chère M.,

The Iris Barry and Rodker stuff is not a compromise but a bet. I stake my critical position, or some part of it, on a belief that both of them *will* do something. I am not risking much, because I have seen a lot of their mss. The Barry has done the draft of a novel, and it has the chance of being literature. Rodker has convinced me, at last, that he "has it in him." And

169

one must have les jeunes. Rodker ought to be up to regulation in a few years time.

He will go farther than Richard Aldington, though I don't expect anyone to believe that statement for some time. He has more invention, more guts. His father did not have a library full of classics, but he will learn.

They are neither of them STUPID, blockheaded as Flint and Lawrence are stupid and blockheaded. Lawrence had less showing above the water line when Hueffer took him up than Rodker has now. And certainly Hueffer has been justified. Much as Lawrence annoys me, and inferior as he is to Joyce.

. . . YES the Seven Arts is slop. YES. And the New Republic is dung dust, with an admixture of dung, also dust dry.

I must get out of the big stick habit, and begin to put my prose stuff into some sort of possibly permanent form, not merely into saying things which everybody will believe in three years time and take as a matter of course in ten.

I. E. articles which can be reduced to "Joyce is a writer, GODDAMN your eyes, Joyce is a writer, I tell you Joyce etc. etc." Lewis can paint, Gaudier knows a stone from a milk-pudding. WIPE your feet!!!!!

Dear M. C. A.,

A plague of potato bugs does not call for a counteracting movement in literary criticism, neither is there any use in trying to combat one form of idiotic and pompous solemnity by assuming the mannerisms of the Times Lit. Sup.

Mr. Aldington's article on Joyce in the English Review is the funniest thing that has appeared in England for some time; if he does not succeed in succeeding Edmond Gosse, he at any rate ousts Mr. Owen Seaman, and for this clever bit of sewer cleaning he certainly shd. receive a pension from the ever just British Govt.

The Dean of English criticism, Mr. T. S. Eliot, pronounces that "the greatest poets have been concerned with moral values"; this red-herring is justifiable on the grounds of extreme mental or physical exhaustion. The "greatest of poets" (Herr Je! what a phrase) have also eaten food, walked—and, mehercule, walked upon *legs*. The statements are of about equal value, my own having perhaps a greater per centum of truth in them, a, let us say, 99¼% and should therefore be the more welcome to cautious and scholarly minds.

Aeschylus was concerned in proving that the gods were a bad lot, Oedipus got a rotten deal, etc. Villon is "concerned," I should worry. Shakespeare dramatized some of Montaigne's superficialities, and did perhaps, in Hamlet, indulge in a little Vale Owenism, but the question of survival of personality is metaphysical rather than ethical.

And in any case, in anny kase, in enny case, it is bunkum to drag these matters into a question of poetry.

A work of art, one ought almost to call it an "act of art," is enjoyable in proportion as the maker has made it to please himself.

By this test you can sort out the real from the academic; and I'm hanged if it isn't the only test that leads one through the labyrinth; that enables one to reject, on grounds, the floods of rubbish poured over one, the floods of rubbish which conform to very defined excellence of the definers; of the academics.

(And now, gentlemen, now that the broken eggs and brickbats lie thickly upon the platform, I may perhaps be permitted to continue.)

Even in the "greatest" (for God's sake let us say "longest" if it refers to literature, and "largest" if it refers to painting, and "bulkiest" if to sculpture) . . . works the live part is the part which the artist has put there to please himself, and the dead part is the part which he has put there for some other reason . . ; which he has put there, let us say, because he thinks he *ought* to—i. e., either to get or to *keep* an audience; or to conform to some standard of culture, or to avoid a "vulgarity," or to please a cult (ethical, religious or arty).

When the idea of duty comes in, pleasure ceases. This simple statement is as true of art as amours.

Precisely, a work of art made to please the artist may be comic (unintentionally comic), it may be agreste, barbaric, even stupid (as Montaigne and Dürer and Montecelli are, often, stupid) but it will not be *dead*. It will not have the distinguishing moribund character of a review in the Times, or of the poems in my volume "Canzoni."

＊　　＊　　＊　　＊　　＊　　＊

Christmas came. No money came.

We had planned the most beautiful Christmas of our lives in the gold room. But the last number of the L. R. had been burned by the Post Office and all our money had gone into its publication. We hadn't enough left to buy a Christmas tree. We had no fruits or cakes or candies or nuts or wine or cigarettes. We had no presents for each other. Monday was Christmas Eve.

We counted on something in the post Monday morning. Jane was convinced that her family would send money as usual. I went downstairs at nine o'clock to collect their letters. There was nothing in the box but an illustrated catalogue of mausoleums. (It wouldn't be funny if it weren't true.) It was a de luxe catalogue, illustrated in color. We had a certain pleasure in examining it.

Our luncheon was a little sad. Still we had enough wood for the fire and the room was exquisite. We didn't entirely despair as there was another mail at two o'clock. If Jane's money came she was to give me a dollar and a half to buy my present for her—a blue bottle I had already chosen at Wanamaker's in the old glass department.

Jane went down for the letters at two. There was one from her family. She came running upstairs and tore it open. Yes they were sending a check. But they had forgotten to enclose it.

Three o'clock and Jane said: "I'm going out." She looked stricken. I knew she was going to Wanamaker's glass department. I knew that she was Scandinavian enough in spite of our catastrophes to have hoarded a dollar and that she would spend it on a present for me. I was American enough to have laid by no provision.

If you're clever enough to have some money I beg you to give it to me. I want my present for you more than anything. It's been put aside for me.

So has mine for you, said Jane.

Well, let's spend your dollar for a tree and renounce presents for each other. We don't need them. The room and a tree are enough.

No, said Jane, and went down the stairs.

(Jane tells the story differently—and better. She says that I urged her to go out and buy her present, knowing it would be for me. Not true.)

I paced through the house. I knew no one from whom I could borrow a dollar and a half. Something had to happen. I tried to make it happen by the force of thinking. I sat down on the piano stool to concentrate. And as if this were not a ridiculous idea something did happen. The doorbell rang. Two people came up the stairs. They were anarchists who wanted to subscribe to the L. R. A subscription was a dollar and a half. Vive the anarchists!

It was just four o'clock and I begged my benefactors to excuse me, explaining the necessity for glass. I ran to Wanamaker's.

Jane and I returned about the same time, each with a square box containing blue glass. We shut ourselves up in secrecy and each achieved an elegantly wrapped present. These we put on her mantelpiece and sat down before the fire to contemplate them in true Christmas Eve spirit. Then Cæsar arrived from nowhere with five dollars for a tree. We ran out to Third Avenue, bought a tree and trimmings, a turkey, a bottle of wine, and little cakes. We spent the night in arrangements and the next morning a large box arrived from Chicago, containing every known Christmas need.

* * * * * *

In February Ezra sent us the first chapter of a manuscript he recommended highly, saying he had no idea if we would care to print it as it would probably involve us in difficulties with the censors.

I began the manuscript. I came upon:

Ineluctable modality of the visible: at least that if no more, thought through my eyes. Signatures of all things I am here to read, seaspawn and seawrack, the nearing tide. . . .

174

This is the most beautiful thing we'll ever have, I cried. We'll print it if it's the last effort of our lives.

James Joyce's "Ulysses" began in the *Little Review* in March, 1918. We ran it month after month for three years and four times the issues containing it were burned by order of the United States Post Office, because of alleged obscenity.

It was like a burning at the stake as far as I was concerned. The care we had taken to preserve Joyce's text intact; the worry over the bills that accumulated when we had no advance funds; the technique I used on printer, bookbinders, paper houses—tears, prayers, hysterics or rages—to make them push ahead without a guarantee of money; the addressing, wrapping, stamping, mailing; the excitement of anticipating the world's response to the literary masterpiece of our generation . . . and then a notice from the Post Office: BURNED.

Besides, for many months—for years, to be exact—we had a minimum response from the world's intellectuals about the masterpiece. Almost no one seemed to like it. A desultory appreciation came in from time to time—usually from the far west! New York was particularly cold. The *New York Times* was the worst. We could never insert a word of publicity about "Ulysses" in its literary columns. Indeed the *Times* took pleasure in insulting us roundly as purveyors of lascivious literature. The *Herald-Tribune* was almost as bad. Its literary section was directed at that time by Burton Rascoe. To excuse his utter negligence of "Ulysses"—his definite reservations against it—

he announced (two years later) that we published it incompletely, spasmodically, in a version unrelated to Joyce's original text. Jane retorted in the L. R. that Rascoe wouldn't recognize the Sphinx outside of Egypt.

* * * * * *

I have been amused by Gilbert Seldes' estimate of H. L. Mencken as the influence that all young men of the generation found easy, inevitable and delightful to follow. It would have been difficult for us to follow any of the precepts of the Menckenian mind. Aside from his stand on free speech, which all intelligent people seem to share—though why on earth should speech be free unless it is interesting?—Mencken has championed nothing that the exceptional mind seeks out by instinct. Jane wrote of him in the L. R.:

It is amusing to play with the idea of challenging Mr. Mencken to explain some of his recent statements and to produce his superior, secret artists.

He has never known the creative artist as a fellow artist . . . of all the first-raters that I know I don't know one who would just naturally send his best or strongest work to Mencken . . . that is a part of the thing that makes them first-raters. Somewhere Mencken tells just how cagey he has always been about accepting mss. . . . does he think that the artists have been less cagey in sending him their work?

Also—right here let us take up the herd of perfect "woodsawing" artists loose somewhere between here and Chicago, known only to Mencken. "There is a group which says little and saws woods . . . they are sophisticated, disillusioned, free from cant . . . out of this dispersed, ill-defined group, I believe something will come." Of course disillusion, sophistication, freedom from cant is a pretty poor recipe for the creative artist, but all sorts of things are done: cripples' races, blind juggling, etc. There are no unknown geniuses, there is no artist anywhere unknown to other artists . . . this is one of the simplest axioms about the nature of the artist. If Mr. Mencken can pull artists out of the middle west he must use the same formula as the magician with his rabbit. But I'm not doubting that they "saw wood."

When Mencken endorses I feel much the same delight in his criterion as I feel when a salesperson assures me that "they are the smartest—I wear them myself." I should like to know from some Mencken fan just how many first-rank things he has fought for, how many truly bad he has fought? He has seemed to me to be oblivious to, or afraid of, first-rate men and things. He has been fighting steadily for fifteen years people who had no fight in them, who would have believed all he had to say, at the end of fifteen years.

I have certainly witnessed none of this influx of good material. During the *Little Review's* history we accepted, as nearly as I remember, from the tide of unsolicited manuscripts, just two talents. One was a boy from Detroit, writing under the name of Jitro, whose stories had the realism of canvases of certain young American painters given to painting the bleakness of mining towns. The other was a woman—perhaps the only figure of our generation who deserves the epithet extraordinary.

One day while Jane was alone in the office this extraordinary person walked in. She walked slowly but impressively, with authority and a clanking of bracelets. She saluted Jane with a detached How do you do, but spoke no further and began strolling about the room, examining the contents of the bookshelves. She wore a red Scotch plaid suit with a kilt hanging just below the knees, a bolero jacket with sleeves to the elbows and arms covered with a quantity of ten-cent-store bracelets—silver, gilt, bronze, green and yellow. She wore high white spats with a band of decorative furniture braid around the top. Hanging from her bust were two tea-balls from which the nickel had worn away. On her head was a black velvet tam o' shanter with a feather and several spoons—long ice-cream-soda spoons. She had enormous earrings of tarnished silver and on her hands were many rings, on the little finger high peasant buttons filled with shot. Her hair was the color of a bay horse.

Finally she bestowed her attention upon Jane.

I have sent you a poem, she trumpeted.

Yes, said Jane, pulling out a manuscript signed Tara Osrik.

How you know I write that poem?

I am not entirely without imagination, said Jane.

My real name is another thing. I write it out for you.

She sat down and with extreme ceremony, the peasant buttons ringing like bells, wrote "Baroness Elsa von Freytag von Loringhoven."

We're taking the poem, explained Jane. It's beautiful.

Yes, it is beautiful. I give you others too.

She then expressed her opinion of the *Little Review*—

"the only magazine of art that is art"—and went majestically down the stairs carrying concealed about her person five dollars' worth of two-cent stamps which had been lying on the table. Knowing her as we did later, it is safe to assume that she used them not for postal but for decorative purposes.

We always called her The Baroness. Her history had been dramatic. She had come to New York to the Ritz with the late Baron von Loringhoven, who hurried back to Germany at the outbreak of the war and then, not liking war, shot himself—an act which his wife characterized as the bravest of his life. After the Ritz The Baroness drifted from one adventure to another. Tired of conventional living, she became an artist's model. Tired of conventional dressing, she began creating costumes which resulted in her arrest whenever she appeared upon the streets. Tired of official restraint, she leaped from patrol wagons with such agility that policemen let her go in admiration. Finally, tired of not eating, she found work in a cigarette factory where she provoked such wrath that one of her co-workers in a rage reminiscent of Bizet knocked out two of her side teeth. Oddly enough this did not detract from her distinction.

During these later years she lived in a tenement of two rooms with three dogs. She wrote or painted all day and all night, produced art objects out of tin foil, bits of rubbage found in the streets, beads stolen from the ten-cent

179

store. She considered that she was at the summit of her art period.

The first poem she gave us was dedicated to Marcel Duchamps, who painted the "Nude Descending the Staircase":

Mustir

The sweet corners of thine tired mouth Mustir
So world-old tired   tired to nobility
To more   to shame   to hatred of thineself
So noble soul   so weak a body
Thine body is the prey of mice

The sweet corners of thine tired mouth   Mustir
Undo thine sin. Thine pain is killed in play
Thine body's torture stimulates in play
And silly little bells of perfect tune
Ring in thine throat
Thou art a country devasted   bare   Mustir
Exhausted soil with sandy trembling hills
No food   no water   and ashamed of it
Thou shiver   and an amber-yellow sun
Goes down the horizon
Thou art desert with mirages which drive the mind insane
To walk   and die   a-starving.

About this time, or rather before I believe, we published Djuna Barnes' story, "A Night Among the Horses." Djuna and the *Little Review* began a friendship which might have been great had it not been that Djuna always felt some fundamental distrust of our life—of our talk.

Her intense maternity covered the resentment for the first year or so.

You two poor things, she would say in her warm laughing voice. You're both crazy of course, God help you. I suppose I can stand it if you can, but someone ought to look out for you.

She looked out for us by bringing in the first strawberries of spring and the last oysters of winter, but to the more important luxuries of the soul she turned an unhearing ear. Djuna would never talk, she would never allow herself to be talked to. She said it was because she was reserved about herself. She wasn't, in fact, reserved—she was unenlightened. This led her into the construction of self-myths which she has never taken the pains to revise. Only this year she said to me in Paris:

Well, I like my inside much better than my outside, don't you?

Certainly not. I think your outside is often stunning and I think you don't know anything about your inside.

I may know nothing about it but it's very nice.

How can you know it's nice when you don't know what it's like?

There you go again. There's no talking with you.

For her there was always no talking with us. For us there was no way of establishing a communication with her. It embarrassed her to approach impersonal talk about the personal element. It embarrassed us to attempt a relationship with anyone who was not on speaking terms with her own psyche. Her mind has no abstract facets. She is impatient of such facets, suspicious of them. The Baroness' mind was of the opposite mold. She would adhere, abstractly, to any subject for three days without exhausting it. When *we* were exhausted—having other things to do, such as publishing a magazine—she would revenge herself against our locked doors by strewing tin cans down the stairs, hurling terrible and guttural curses over her shoulder for three flights.

The Baroness didn't appreciate Djuna's work.

I cannot read your stories, Djuna Barnes, she said. I don't know where your characters come from. You make them fly on magic carpets—what is worse, you try to make pigs fly.

Djuna didn't appreciate the Baroness at first. Later she gave her work a grudging admiration. Much later she accepted it as perhaps the best of any woman's of our time. In the Baroness' last tragic period—when everyone else, worn out with her, felt resourceless before the havoc her mere existence caused, Djuna's maternity came to the rescue and sustained the Baroness for two years in Paris. It was to Djuna that Elsa von Loringhoven wrote the letters from Germany published last year in the L. R. and in *Transition* and described by that periodical as "the saddest and most beautiful letters in English literature." I quote a passage taken from *Transition* and from the last number of the *Little Review*.

I will probably—yes, yes, yes, probably *have* to die. When life is not, one has to die. . . . I cannot any more conceive of the idea of a decent artist existence for me, and another is not possible. . . . I have come into this situation and all entangles itself in this indescribable way to my discredit and destruction at last— only because I am I, and no other person, another person wouldn't have come into it. . . . My terror is so genuine, so must my end be. Life goes out of life . . . and I marvel that I have been in it—and I see myself treading again this earth with an ardent heart. . . . I feel my mind becoming shaded, as I live in dark shade! I cast around, and to my utter consternation— that torpor that enthralls me—there is nothing but icy stare— out of all my rich life. . . . At this time of my life I should be covered with garlands—and I stand denuded for shame. How shall I go through? . . . Dark fear is on me, I am not brave enough to bear it all alone. . . . Even for suicide one has to arrange, to go up, to lie down forever. Why must I learn wisdom and perish for it . . . ornaments of my imperishable beauty that is *there* as long as *I am,* smothered by ague now! . . . Let me do art—a little, a little—joyfully with clean conscience of my right. Why not? Why am I condemned and I did nothing but beauty. Goodbye—I am quibbling. Goodbye, though I am afraid. Forgive me my troubled being. . . . I am not truly deranged even, but scattered. . . . Tragedy is written on me—stigmatizing me —people, dull as they are, perceive it—they are never *too dull* to disapprove of something different from themselves—also to fear it. . . . I almost despise myself for the trouble I make and the trouble that troubles me. But what shall I do? I am stunned nearly to exhaustion. Forgive me, but I am mourning destruction of high quality—as I know myself to be. . . . That is the tragedy—I still feel deep in me glittering wealth. . . .

* * * * * *

It was late spring and we had a nostalgia for the country. A charming Chicago woman who spent several years

trying to preserve her admiration of us in spite of
"Ulysses," invited us to week-end in Bellport, Long Island
—a dormant village with a few smart hotels whose chief
claim to our attention was its proximity to an even more
dormant village called Brookhaven.

Brookhaven, Long Island, was a mile from the sea. Its
roads were white, made of a long accumulation of shells.
Its air was made of mists. Its trees were old and quiet. Its
houses were white, with red geraniums in the windows.
Its post office was on a brook and combined mail with groceries, with Mr. Valentine and Mr. Reeves disseminating
the village gossip over the counters. Its fields were full of
water oats. Its bridges spanned a rich vegetation of sea gar-
dens, with lilies on the surface and a slowly waving moss
underneath. Its autumns were full of ducks' cries and the
long wailings of migratory birds.

That first day I came by accident upon the village and
upon a small house. Its abandoned doorstep faced the sea.
Its abandoned interior faced utter ruin. The floors were
falling through and the walls were nothing but holes in
the plaster. On one side of it was a sunken river, filled with
reeds that turned toward the sea.

I was alone for the discovery. I sat down on the door-
step. A late sun sifted through the hickory and locust trees.
The locusts were blue, their shadows covered the house.
Jane came along.

This is a house we must take.

I see what you mean, said Jane satisfyingly.

We took it eventually for twelve dollars a month. It

wasn't a house; it was hardly a structure. But being a hundred and twenty-five years old it had an atmosphere and a mystery. The mystery was made by the mists and the submerged river "where dead men sink into the ooze"—the phrase Jane found with which to frighten me.

The lady from Chicago decided to help us achieve this gem. She came out to look it over. One look sufficed.

You can't possibly go into such a proposition, she pronounced. There's nothing here. You'd have to rebuild. Better to take another house.

But it's the rebuilding that attracts us!

In the neighborhood was another old house said to have belonged to the Edwin Booth family, and full of antique furniture which we craved. After certain negotiations (including the family's firm refusal to part with four hideous modern golden oak chairs) we acquired the contents of the house for twenty-five dollars—three beds (mahogany, four poster), two chests of drawers, fourteen chairs, three armchairs, three mahogany tables, rag carpet and rugs, a kitchen stove, andirons, and a priceless service of old flat silver.

Our passion for broken-down objects led us to purchase (for five dollars) a damaged gypsy van which we placed in the front yard, swathed in mosquito netting, and used as a residence while rebuilding the house. Except for the fireplaces we did it all—plastering, carpentry, floors. We had brought from New York seeds, flowers, plants, and animals—six yellow chickens just hatched and two little yellow ducks in the same condition. One of the ducks expired slowly in my hands a week later. This was the beginning of a series of animal dramas in Brookhaven—a white cat (half-angora, half-mad); a white angora rabbit, unnamed but of tragic destiny; two white pigeons; and a little brown rabbit unknown to us but fated to haunt us for many days and nights.

Once established, we stayed too long. The sad late autumn was irresistible and we spent days roasting ducks with all the ceremony of Christmas feasts, and talking of everything from the holes in psychoanalysis to the sick spine visible in Scriabine's music.

We returned to New York after Thanksgiving. The months in Brookhaven had given us an unharassed period in which to develop new psychological material and we went about talking as usual but with more than usual exuberance. We could find the Achilles heel in everybody's psychic set-up—the psychoanalysts were inferior sleuths compared to us. We stuck pins into people. I felt that in this we were doing a necessary world's work. As for Jane, she never had the sardonic pleasure in it that was often attributed to her. She regarded the pricking of the bubbles of self-illusion—helping people to distinguish between wish-fulfillment and reality—an essential to the race. I went further. I assumed that people were dying for such treatment, that they hailed Jane's profound observation as salutary. I always did. When she resorted to analyzing me and came upon facts too scathing to be spoken she would put them in a letter, under my door. It is certainly more painful to be pinned in a letter than in a conversation—the telling phrase leaps out at you in a way that takes your breath. I always liked this. Jane still tells how, hoping to have reduced my self-esteem to a pulp, she would see a look of exaltation spread over my face:

Never forget what you wrote in this note. It's too good. You must try to put it into the *Little Review*.

Being really solicitous about human development, Jane sometimes found this impersonality of mine discouraging. But I am eternally interested in performance.

Margaret carries me about under her arm like a fighting cock, Jane used to say, and throws me into every ring she sees. And she sees nothing but rings.

Not only rings but circles—and vicious. For instance, we used to develop headaches trying to understand why we found it so hard to relate our talents to money-making. It is not strange that talented people without practical abilities or common sense live and die without money. But since our practical capacities extended from the production of biscuits to the construction of houses and our super good sense was often attested to by financiers, impresarios, publishers, lawyers who predicted a doubling of their business if they could hire our brains—we could never discover why no one would endow us. We had been offered endowments but always on the condition that we

187

would make the *Little Review* the kind of mediocre journal we particularly detested.

Israel Solon—another of my favorite talkers—explained our difficulties like this:

You're too arrogant. At least you appear arrogant. You appear to have everything. People don't like this. Feeling they can give you nothing important that you haven't already, their only revenge is to keep money from you. This at least leaves them a certain position in their relation to you.

Our effect upon people may be one of arrogance. We are not arrogant. No one who is simple is arrogant. From my point of view no one can even feel arrogant who must live for months without her favorite perfume.

Christmas comes quickly for those who fear it. This time we planned to meet it without high hopes and with a little money. We accomplished neither.

But we took the situation calmly and spent the day reading. We had a Christmas tree. We even had three—a small one with a smaller one on either side, completing the design.

At tea time a tall blond man arrived, introduced himself as J. S. Watson of the *Dial,* and said he wanted to buy a copy of Eliot's "Prufrock." We had published most of the poems in this collection and kept the book on sale. It cost seventy-five cents. Mr. Watson gave me a dollar bill, took the book and left, saying: "Oh no, I don't want any change." As I put the dollar away I chanced to look at it.

It was a hundred-dollar bill. I ran after Mr. Watson to tell him he had made a mistake.

Oh no, he said again, so embarrassed that he began falling down the stairs. I brought it for the *Little Review*. It's good, I assure you.

I made him come back and talk. We became friends and so remained during all our attacks on the *Dial* as "a de-alcoholized version of the *Little Review*." Watson came several times with his salutary hundred-dollar bill which kept the magazine alive when otherwise it would have succumbed. As Jane said, he knew a good magazine when he saw one.

In the evening the anarchists—Emma Goldman, Berkman, and followers—came in to see our tree. The comrades rushed into the gold room as if crashing through bars. The stampede left us trembling. Before leaving one of them asked if he couldn't take one of the smaller trees with him. Jane looked troubled but found the courage to refuse.

I'm sorry, I should love to give it to you but . . . it's part of the design.

They filed out, puzzled.

Emma Goldman asked me to lend our Fourteenth Street office to the comrades for a series of meetings about the war. I hated to do it, knowing that we would probably fall into trouble with the conservative Van Buren estate. I hesitated shamefully for a day. But E.G. reacted to the hesitation and I was spared the pain of refusing. I met her in the Brevoort and for the first time saw in her face and manner a disappointment in me. She was much too delicate, even where her passion for anarchism was concerned, to override a hesitation. She talked of other things. I was too torn to talk at all. Remembering Jane's carpentry work on the bookshelves, it didn't seem fair to risk losing the office. As it turned out I might as well have offered it to the anarchists, because we lost it anyway. The Van Buren estate disapproved of our private feelings about the world war and asked us to give up the office.

Other anarchists were not so fair-minded as Emma Goldman. I soon heard that Leonard Abbott was broadcasting the opinion that I represented the tragedy of the anarchist movement in America.

*   *   *   *   *   *

We published a hundred dollars' worth of "Ulysses" and settled again into poverty. We had no potatoes this time—a sack of flour was all that remained. Jane made biscuits and for three days we ate nothing else but.

We were becoming ashamed of advertising our poverty. People were kind and had helped too often to be asked again. We never squandered ten cents of the money that was given to the magazine. A great deal of money was not necessary to keep a magazine like the *Little Review* alive, but a certain fixed sum that could be counted upon regularly was essential. It was this we could never achieve.

I hit upon a plan. I would canvass Wall Street for subscriptions. I would urge the brokers to the take the L.R. for themselves and their families. This would extend our cultural influence and enlarge our subscription list. I had tried canvassing in Chicago in the big office buildings. Watchmen, observing my progress from floor to floor, explained that peddling wasn't allowed. I ignored or overruled their protests, converting them to the quality of my merchandise.

In New York I encountered no resistance. I took the subway to the heart of the business district, chose the largest building in sight and began at the top, entering only those doors which bore individual names. I asked for Mr. so and so. What did I want to see him about? An entirely personal matter. I refused to write my name on the proffered pad and put on such a high manner that the office boys or secretaries ushered me in with pride. It is surprising the number of offices I visited, more than surprising the number of subscriptions I managed to get. The procedure was simple:

I very much want you to subscribe to my magazine.

And why should I do that? the well-dressed young broker would ask.

Because it's the most interesting review of modern art published in America to-day.

Well, I might as well take a chance.

If I had had the stamina to continue an effort that was distasteful to me, I might have developed a business out of these hold-up methods. But I couldn't spend my life running through office buildings.

Before the flair died however I made a special call on Frank Vanderlip. He was so unsympathetic that I can't remember how he looked. I have never forgotten a face in my life but of Frank Vanderlip I retain only an impression of gray—or white—hair. I began by telling him I hoped he would subscribe to the *Little Review* and perhaps give us a donation to make our continued existence possible.

I know nothing of the *Little Review*.

Otto Kahn is a subscriber and likes it very much.

Mr. Kahn supports a lot of things that are outside my interests.

We finally fell into a heated and somewhat unpleasant controversy about the necessity for art.

I like to help people who are starving, said Mr. Vanderlip in a tone of finality.

I felt I had come to the right source. But since I didn't look starved I didn't know just how to present my fact. Still I couldn't eat any more biscuits and I hit upon the ingenious argument that the *Little Review* was a living testimony to the truth that man cannot live by bread alone. But Mr. Vanderlip wouldn't follow me into spiritual realms. He spoke of the starving masses in Russia, and our interview ended.

*   *   *   *   *   *

Marguerite D'Alvarez had just come to New York. Her first season, like that of other good European artists arriving unheralded in New York, had been nil. The critics hadn't even discovered that she had a voice in her first Carnegie Hall concert, being put off by what they considered her too-exotic treatment of Debussy.

In the late spring, having no manager to forbid such generosity, she offered to give us a benefit concert in the Provincetown Theatre. We accepted gratefully, thinking more of the pleasure than of the benefit. In fact we became so confused over the issues that before we knew it we had launched posters announcing the benefit concert free of admission. Artists naturally had to be invited— and how tell a man to his face that he wasn't one? (That is, there are times when this is necessary and easy but before the door of a concert hall is perhaps not one of them.) So we had no tickets and the public filled the theatre. Allen Tanner played the accompaniments. D'Alvarez was so striking in her black dress, with black handkerchief, black hair and black eyebrows arched like Chinese dragons, that the audience rose to its feet to greet her. It was probably one of the best concerts she has ever given anywhere.

One of the persons we had most hoped for in the audience was the Baroness. She had been impressively invited and had accepted with enthusiasm, saying she rarely heard music, that it made far too great an impression on her, that she couldn't imagine any woman intelligent enough to sing well, that she couldn't abide prima donnas, but that she would be glad to come and see what she thought. The concert finished and she hadn't appeared.

We had a reception upstairs afterward at Christine's.

People were pouring the usual banalities upon D'Alvarez when a strange figure appeared in the door and a hush fell upon the room. It was Elsa von Freytag von Loringhoven. She wore a trailing blue-green dress and a peacock fan. One side of her face was decorated with a canceled postage stamp (two-cent American, pink). Her lips were painted black, her face powder was yellow. She wore the top of a coal scuttle for a hat, strapped on under her chin like a helmet. Two mustard spoons at the side gave the effect of feathers. Without the slightest self-consciousness, in the dramatic silence that always enveloped her public emergences, she walked directly to D'Alvarez and the two women confronted each other. An enmity had come into the atmosphere. It didn't come from the Baroness.

I had to miss your concert, she announced in her most serious manner (the point being she was serious and expected to be understood) and I am sorry. But it was necessary for me to work on this costume. I came as soon as it was finished.

D'Alvarez misread her entirely—probably thought the Baroness was making fun of her. Her repartee didn't function. The Baroness stood at ease examining the singer as if she were a species of extraordinary interest to her as no doubt D'Alvarez was. Then she pronounced her first judgment.

You are very young, she said engagingly.

D'Alvarez felt it was time to assert herself. She launched into a flow of first-class prima donna talk. The Baroness

194

stood watching her gravely. Finally D'Alvarez wound up with:

My art is for humanity. I sing only for humanity.

The Baroness called out loudly.

I wouldn't lift a leg for humanity!

She turned her back on D'Alvarez and spent the next hour explaining the beauty of her costume to everybody who wanted to listen—which means everybody.

The late spring held for us another adventure of the sympathies—the arrest and trial of Emma Goldman and Alexander Berkman for having urged rebellion against conscription, though their passivism was internationally known. Why hadn't they fought conscription? That would have been the interesting question. They were convicted on the general principles of anarchism, sentenced to two years in prison, fined a thousand dollars each and deportation after their prison term.

We went to the trial every day and lunched with them during the recesses. They were naïvely optimistic at moments that their structure of reason and philosophy would convince any judge of their idealism.

They were charming in court. E.G. was the earnest preacher rather than the fiery fighter, and extremely effective. Berkman was uncontrollably temperamental. He even provoked the judge into displays of temper and fought him man to man in a way the latter seemed to like far better than E.G.'s controlled reasonableness. E.G. addressed him as Your Honor, in a tone which indicated there was nothing else to do about it. But Berkman avoided this, and once when the judge interrupted him his nerves gave way completely, he struck the table before him and cried:

Don't interrupt me—don't interrupt me again or I can't say what I'm trying to say; and it's important.

The judge let him go on to the end without a reprimand.

The anarchists were allowed twenty-four hours after the verdict to close up their affairs and start off for prison. A rich friend of Emma Goldman had reserved a luxurious room in the Belmont Hotel where she might pass a comfortable night before entering the prison sweat-shop where she was to make overalls for two years.

Their fine, I believe, was paid by my favorite enemy, Nineteen Millions. After their two years' imprisonment they sailed for Russia with a thousand dollar gift from the same source. This was stolen from under Berkman's pillow by their comrades, the Soviets.

* * * * * *

After this strenuous episode the *Little Review* moved its headquarters again to Brookhaven.

Our first ill-considered gesture was the acquisition of a newly-born white kitten, scion of a poignant race whose members were all slightly defective. This being their appeal, our choice fell upon the most fragile of the lot. We named her Alice in Wonderland and she became another link in that atmosphere of half-things (mists and shadows and sunken rivers) which made Brookhaven unforgettable.

Next Jane conceived a garden of flowers and vegetables which was to border the river and face the sea. At its far extremity were to be tuberoses. She labored for weeks, digging, planting and thinking interesting thoughts which were to go into a book I was begging her to write. The book never materialized, though the tuberoses did. The little house with its blue floors and pink walls and black tables held stalks of tuberoses that made one faint on entering at twilight. Alice in Wonderland, white and exotic and slightly ailing, walked about on black tables, delicately sniffing white flowers.

Someone had just written a book called "Gardening with Brains"—which suggestive title moved Jane to do a dialogue intended for her book, but which went instead into the *Little Review*.

"GARDENING WITH BRAINS"
by jh

SCENE: *"The Little Review" in summer quarters: tiny house with large garden by the sea.*
CHARACTERS: M. C. A. *and* jh. *jh. working in garden. M. C. A. comes down the lawn dressed in black silk Annette Kellerman, Limited; large white coral beads about neck, bracelets, short hair elaborately trained about elaborately indifferent head.*
jh. Why don't you ever come down and have a look at the garden?

M. C. A. I don't know anything about such things—(*approaches as if entering a ballroom*).—What are these?

jh. Tomatoes.

M. C. A. And these?

jh. Potatoes.

M. C. A. I don't see any.

jh. They grow under the ground.

M. C. A. How exasperating!

(*neurotic silence*)

I don't see how you can keep your interest if everything grows under the ground.

jh. Everything doesn't. Tomatoes grow on top, potatoes under.

M. C. A. Aren't you clever to know such things?

jh. I have to—What would I do if I ever got the seeds mixed and dug into a t-o-m-a-t-o!!!

M. C. A. (*turning to go, with a sweeping gesture*)—Is there anything so charming as a garden by the sea!

jh. (*imitating M. C. A.'s manner*)—Ah! but the sea-weeds!!

Allen Tanner came out to see us. It was amusing to dress in white, carry black sticks and walk formally and decoratively in the garden, followed by Alice making a high fountain of her tail. From these graceful moods we drifted into evenings of Allen's best playing. When there was mist we hung Chinese lanterns in the trees and the soft drip of the moisture fell upon the pink, green and yellow lights while Allen played all the moonlight music of the world.

After this Jane and I entered into a phase of talk and experiment concerning the piano which dominated our summer. There were two things I wanted to analyze fundamentally—the psychology of performance and a new attitude toward the everlasting question of technique.

We argued this way: if you have a brain you know that music played in public is not merely music: it is music plus performance. Performance has nothing to do with practicing in one's room. It is something in relation to an audience. It is another subject. You can never find musicians who are prepared to talk intelligently on this subject. They will talk technique, emotion, professionalism, amateurism, stage fright. Professionalism to them means a perfection of musical technique. It never means what it should: a perfection of human technique.

Musicians are naïve. They still respect a distinction that was once made between feeling and mind. To them an artist is either emotional or mental. They allow for no mentality in the emotional type and vice versa. They had better consort with lion-tamers or music hall headliners and find out a few things. I am not talking about hypnotizing an audience with a fixed eye or a magnetic fluid, nor of holding it spellbound with superfluous gestures, nor of dominating it by an enormous concentration. I am talking about having an attitude, clearly maintained. You never have an attitude toward anything in life until you know a great deal about your psychological make-up. You already know the psychological make-up of any audience: it is in a state waiting to be dominated. And you can't dominate it by thinking vaguely of hypnotism. You can dominate it only by knowing what elements in you can compel attention—by finding out in your everyday life where you hold an auditor's attention, where you lose it.

The problem is the same for a musician as for an after-dinner speaker. Exhibitionism merely means choosing one phase of your personality for conscious and intelligent exploitation. If you are predominantly a lyric person you can compel a lyrical attention. Play Chopin, Schumann, Debussy, Scriabine—play Bach lyrically—and you have your audience. If you are a hard, dry or brilliant person—play fireworks and you have your audience. But have you noticed that when you ask a lyrical person to play Debussy he quickly responds by doing some restricted page of Scarlatti; and if you ask the virtuoso type to play Stravinsky he takes great pleasure in offering an ecstatic and swooning bit of Chopin?

Harold Bauer is the performer par excellence. He is usually billed as "the master pianist." Such a tag means something quite definite. It doesn't mean he plays better than anyone else. It means that people sense in him some knowledge of the human situation between auditor and performer. Bauer knows that you can't make people react emotionally if you yourself are in a state of emotion. You can offer a deliberate calculation toward a deliberate result. If you are doing this you are occupied. You are being conscious, not self-conscious, and you are making your audience conscious of you. This is being a master. Professional pianists go to Bauer's concerts because subconsciously they enjoy his control of an audience. They say: it's such a relief to sit back and relax—Bauer is never nervous.

They mean they are soothed by the chemical experience of being intelligently dominated. These things are fairly obvious and should be taught in all music schools instead of exercises for the fingers. But one doesn't hear it. People are antagonistic to hearing about the thing behind. It destroys their illusions.

A woman once told me of the shock Harold Bauer gave her.

Have you a book here with fairly large print? he asked her.

I've nothing but Dickens.

That will serve.

And she was astounded and not a little horrified to see him place the volume of Dickens on the piano rack and read it, turning its pages deliberately, as he played through his concert program.

She wasn't shocked by a purely musical trick of Casals', with whom she was studying the 'cello. When she couldn't phrase a passage as she wished Casals said:

Sing it. If you can sing it you can play it.

She found this extreme good sense, as indeed it was. But she couldn't see the good sense in Bauer's trick to liberate his mind and emotions from his music in order to leave them free for another preoccupation.

Jane and I began to construct a good sense program of piano technique. I was a good subject, having never been able to follow the precepts given me by any teacher—that is, I could follow them but they seemed to me to mean nothing.

First, we had to establish how small a part the hand and fingers play in piano technique. Second, how small a part practice plays in acquiring technique. Practice is a stupid thing. Painters don't practice—they paint. Poets don't practice—they make up poems. They correct, revise, or reconceive, but they don't sit doing the same thing over and over for hours, days, months. One might practice, over and over, one's relations with an audience. But it is silly—supremely silly—to sit and practice the piano. I partake of this silliness.

Play, said Jane. Don't sit. A hen sits.

Of course I wanted to correct this propensity, knowing it to be laziness, emotional leakage, and in some way comparable to learning about life only by experience. This I do not do. I decide what an experience should be and try to make it come out that way. But on the piano I prefer to live through the experience of finding out what will happen by doing the same experiment over and over. One ought to begin at the other end. Begin with a conception of form and the result is assured.

Jane knows the human anatomy; so she helped me to relate the body to a conception of form. Something like this: you can learn to play tennis in two ways—you can practice a conception of form and miss hitting the ball until you've mastered the form, after which you'll always hit the ball; or you can strive only to hit the ball and let this decide what your form will be. It may be something very ugly. It has been said that when a movement is based on necessity it is beautiful. You may prefer to say that when a movement is based on beauty it will be necessary. Necessity may be the mother of invention; invention is certainly the mother of luxury. The invention of "form" inevitably leads to beauty. This is a more exciting angle from which to approach any task, any art.

I tried therefore to begin with a conception of how the body should look in order to function most beautifully. We talked about the look of a musical passage, never about its feel. If the curve of a certain emotion was large it should be taken with a large muscle, or from a large base. Jane watched me, sketched me, and I practiced appearance— comparable to the intricate adjustments of a man on horseback. One could probably learn to ride a bicycle or walk a tight rope without any practice whatever if one's idea of the "form" of it were precise enough.

Of course it wasn't easy to put these theories into practice. There were days when I despaired of achieving anything—days when I wept—days that I startled Jane by screaming: Where *is* my upper arm? or insisting that I had no shoulder blades.

But such work seemed, and seems, necessary to me. Most men pianists look as if they were sitting at sewing machines. But how many women pianists are there who don't look positively offensive sitting on one hip, the other poised in the air; sitting low with the arms bent up like hooks; sitting too close; sitting like Ethel Leginska with the look of a wounded bird. Busoni knew how to sit triumphantly. Paderewski sits scornfully. Bauer sits masterfully. I don't understand how people can continue going to concerts which offer them nothing for the attention of the mind. An engineer without any sense of music could watch Bauer's playing for hours with interest.

*   *   *   *   *   *

With the autumn Alice in Wonderland became a problem. Considering her health, it was impossible to keep her in the city. We realized that we ought to treat the problem scientifically; ought to believe that the span of a single summer had been for her a perfect life.

Jane undertook to chloroform her. We buried her under a locust tree and left for New York.

But we couldn't sleep, and the next morning I found a note from Jane saying that she had gone back to Brookhaven. I took the first train possible and arrived as the sun was going down. I found Jane kneeling before the fire, holding Alice in her hands. She had dug up the kitten and for hours had been trying to revive it.

Cats have nine lives, she assured me.

But her look was strange and I was frightened.

*   *   *   *   *   *

Another winter of poverty in New York loomed ahead of us. I was tiring. For one thing, being undernourished, I was seized with an increasing and uncontrollable thirst for candy. When it became undeniable I would go walking with Jane, lure her into a drug store, and approach the cashier's desk.

Will you be kind enough to lend me a dime for carfare? I find I've forgotten to bring any money with me.

This always worked, as it probably would in no other country in the world. Certainly not in France, where Hart Crane, one of our early contributors, was arrested this year for having lacked one franc on his bill of five francs in a Montparnasse café. Even when strangers offered to pay it for him, with a carelessness for money remarkable in this country, the *patronne* insisted on calling the police for the principle of the thing; and when Hart felt that the situation demanded a little exaggerated action and gave the policeman a rather exaggerated tap on the jaw, he was taken off to jail for five days. After which he was given a trial and had to pay a hunred-franc fine. All of which shows that it's safer to live in New York where everyone is good-natured about dimes.

With my dime from the drug store I would go to the nearest candy shop and buy chocolates. (I always repaid the dime as soon as possible.) Sometimes I invaded a smart candy shop, asked for the manager, explained that I was uptown without any money but with an irresistible longing for candy. I suggested that he lend me twenty-five cents, which I would repay the next day, but which I would immediately expend for his best caramels. He always seemed happy to meet this demand. Life is not so difficult after all.

Jane, I noticed, was happily nourished by these foragings. But she said she didn't approve of them.

I wouldn't mind so much, she grumbled, if you didn't go in looking like a queen and come out looking like a baby.

This was the winter of my discontent. Tired of having no clothes, tired of being continually ugly, I dressed for dinner in the apartment in the only becoming garment I had left—a crêpe de chine chemise. Draped in an old fur scarf and installed before the fire, I enjoyed the décolleté and talked better for the illusion of charm.

*   *   *   *   *   *

A letter from Ezra put us in touch with his great friend, John Quinn, and brought us good fortune.

John Quinn was New York's most distinguished Tammany lawyer who had built up a reputation and a fortune through hard work and the fighting spirit of the Irish. He fought everybody, from his office boys—who trembled visibly and were in consequence the most inefficient office boys in the world—to his friend and protégé, James Joyce, who sat calmly in Paris and ignored Quinn's cutting suggestions as to how "Ulysses" ought to be written.

I've told Joyce and Pound and Lewis not to write to me for six weeks. Sick and tired of their foolishness.

One wanted to ask why six weeks exactly. But John

Quinn continued to imprecate Joyce and Pound in a voice of frenzied anger, followed by a beaming smile of satisfaction over his six-weeks' prohibition, and, before a week had passed followed by a check—to insure their keeping him *au courant* with their troubles.

John Quinn spent his fortune for modern art and had the best collection of Brancusi in America. We went to dine with him in his apartment, Central Park West. Every inch of space from baseboard to ceiling was covered with modern painting and sculpture. Brancusi's "Child in the World" stood out grotesquely in the confusion. Walt Kuhn was there. Quinn began quarreling about an article in the *New Republic* that week which had labeled a certain man intellectual but not intelligent.

How can a man be intellectual and not intelligent? Intelligent but not intellectual I can see, but the other way round—well, they're crazy.

I suggested that since intelligence might be considered a native quality and intellectuality an attainment, a man might well possess the latter without a trace of the former. This most obvious explanation seemed to soothe him. He left the quarreling possibilities of that subject and sought another.

I've been thinking a great deal about the *Little Review*. You want to bring it up to scratch. You want the public to think you've got plenty of money. 'We're a going concern. Get aboard.' That's the note. Nobody's business that you're poor. Make them think you're rich. And that's nobody's business either. Keep people off. Keep them guessing. A man came into my office the other day and said: 'Well, Mr. Quinn, you seem to be making a lot of money.' I said to him: 'And you seem to be talking about what's none of your damned business.' Ha, ha, ha—that's the way to fix them.

I suggested that we did in fact keep up the appearances, that what troubled us, rather, was how to keep up the fires: that we had recently been reduced to burning paper instead of wood—that the appearance was all right, the reality a little short of convincing.

I've done that, said Walt Kuhn. You can roll the paper pretty tight and it will burn a lot longer than you think.

A good idea, said John Quinn, looking pleased. I did it when I was a boy.

He went off into gales of happy laughter.

John Quinn spent the rest of the evening telling us how we ought to run the *Little Review*. His advice was excellent—anyone with a fortune could have followed it.

Two days later, having given me no hint that he meant to help us, he sent a letter announcing that he was arranging to endow the L.R. to the extent of sixteen hundred dollars.

We nearly found ourselves ill, as the French say. Mr. Quinn himself was contributing four hundred dollars and asking three other people to do the same—Otto Kahn, Mrs. James Byrne, and Max Pam of Chicago. There would be no strings attached to the gifts. Mr. Kahn already knew us and, though he insisted he was too old-fashioned to follow all our ideas, had given us small donations with which to publish those ideas. To Mrs. Byrne and Mr. Pam John Quinn wrote a eulogy of the *Little Review* that surprised us. All three responded and we started a bank account with sixteen hundred dollars.

With this we brought out the magazine regularly and slept at night without fear of bills in the morning. For the first time in our history we had leisure to improve our format, adopt striking typography, and plan publicity campaigns. For at least eight months we lived and worked without panic.

That winter New York had an epidemic of influenza—to which we both succumbed—and something worse than an epidemic of property loss—a change of property laws or some other crisis which I never understood. The only feature of it which was clear was that our landlord lost the Sixteenth Street house and we had to move. I will pass over the agony of losing the gold room. Jane said she was going to slash its walls with black paint so that no one else could use it. She didn't.

We found a small apartment on the top floor of the house which held the Washington Square Bookshop, at 27 West Eighth Street. We decided to do no special decorating this time and almost kept our word. We did one room in unrelieved black, with a magenta floor and a midnight blue rug.

Otherwise the only striking event of that year was the apparition of the Baroness with her head shaved.

Elsa von Loringhoven had had a tragic spring. William Carlos Williams, one of our contributors, had found her poetry interesting and had called to tell her so. Incidentally he took her a basket of peaches. They talked. The Baroness found him charming and fell violently in love with him. Williams didn't want her in love with him and became thoroughly frightened at the avalanche.

He might have stopped it by treating her like a human being (as Marcel Duchamp did) and convincing her that it was no use. But instead he acted like a small boy and wrote her insulting letters in which his panic was all too visible. He said such stupid things in these letters (all of which, including her infinite pages of replies, we had to hear read aloud in a strong voice), and gave her such opportunities to refute all his ideas, that we began to despair ever of getting out the next number of the L.R. We had no time left, after listening, and no space left after putting the letters on file. She considered the correspondence important—it exposed the case of the American man.

He brought me peaches and now he won't look at me. Not just peaches—they were ripe peaches. Are American men really so naïve as that?

She didn't give up her struggle for Williams until she had frightened him to the point of planning an escape to Europe. She went to New Jersey to the suburban town where he lived and installed herself in his car which was usually standing at the curb on spring nights to take him on emergency calls—Williams being also a doctor. One night he came out to rush to a maternity case and found the Baroness romantically waiting in the front seat.

I thought we could have a real talk, she told us afterward—meaning a conversation of at least three hours.

She ignored his professional obligation and finally Williams threatened to call the police. She stopped him with a royal gesture:

I'll tell the *Little Review* on you.

She never forgave him for not listening to her. He was a coward. He was ignoble. He didn't know what she might have made of him. He might have become a great man. Now he would have to live and die without learning anything.

At last when she could struggle no more she had to think of something else to do. So she shaved her head. Next she lacquered it a high vermilion. Then she stole the crêpe from the door of a house of mourning and made a dress of it.

She came to see us. First she exhibited the head at all angles, amazing against our black walls. Then she jerked off the crêpe with one movement.

It's better when I'm nude, she said.

It was very good. But we were just as glad that some of our more conservative friends didn't choose that moment to drop in.

Shaving one's head is like having a new love experience, proclaimed the Baroness.

Complaints about "Ulysses" continued to pour in. We were becoming inured to the most insulting, the most offensive, the most vulgar letters telling us exactly what the public thought of James Joyce. During the summer in Brookhaven I received a letter voicing the general indignation caused by Episode XIII—the episode in which Mr. Bloom indulges in simple erotic musings about Gerty McDowell. It also heralded the difficulties we were to have almost immediately with the Society for the Suppression of Vice.

Judging by the handwriting on the envelope I felt that the letter was going to be particularly charming. I have never recovered from my early fixation about beautiful handwriting. This had the look of a ship on the sea. I opened the letter and prepared to be charmed. I quote it because it is typical of hundreds we received:

I think this is the most damnable slush and filth that ever polluted paper in print. I have persisted in reading it to the end. I wanted to know why those responsible for printing what the authorities condemned should jeopardize their own reputations unless there was something intrinsically beautiful even though misunderstood by the censors. And so, as I say, I persisted in reading to the bitter end of Episode XIII. Damnable, hellish filth from the gutter of a human mind born and bred in contamination. There are no words I know to describe, even vaguely, how disgusted I am; not with the mire of his effusion but with all those whose minds are so putrid that they dare allow such muck and sewage of the human mind to besmirch the world by repeating it—and in print, through which medium it may reach young minds. Oh my God, the horror of it.

With all the force of my being I reject thinking of you as part of this hellish business. I loathe the possibility of your continuing to associate yourself with such degradation. It defies all that is moderate in speaking of it. No one connected in any measure, or having any part or parcel with a person who could know such filth, think such . . . but what is the use? It pollutes one to speak of it, even to cry out against it. I hate, I loathe, I detest the whole thing and everything connected with it. It has done something tragic to my illusions about America. How could you?

I sat up all night to write an answer—such was my hurt for Joyce, my own hurt.

Djuna Barnes who was visiting us couldn't understand the hurt.

Mart the Obscure, she said. Why do you care? Whatever you do don't answer that letter.

Don't answer? mocked Jane. She will not only answer, she'll argue. The editor of the *Little Review* has never been interested in preserving the dignity of life.

Of course I answered, evidently effectively, for I received an apology by return post. I began by saying:

You received a copy of the *Little Review* at your own request. This was a tacit agreement to deal with it courteously. You received it from me. You have heard me speak of James Joyce with reverence. And yet you did not hesitate to speak of him to me with grossness. You know that I regard his work as the

213

high water-mark of the literature of to-day; you know also that in five minutes an analyst of half my skill could unmask your profound ignorance of all branches of art, science, life. On what then is your temerity toward me based? It is not important that you dislike James Joyce. It is as it should be. He is not writing for you. He is writing for himself and for the people who care to find out how life has offended and hurt him.

Then I explained that only a person who has been "crucified on his sensibilities" would write as Joyce writes of his experiences with mankind and with nature. I explained that only a very exceptional man could revenge himself on the banality, the aridity, the obscenity from which he had suffered by transcribing it so flawlessly into an epic criticism of mankind. I explained everything that one should never trouble to explain to the people who understand nothing.

But since I had no way of hitting out at all the obscene letters of criticism that reached me I felt that this one could serve as an example. I became obsessed with the necessity of forcing someone to apologize to James Joyce and to me.

The apology I received was not based upon any new understanding of Joyce's work. It was an admission of having written without temperance and thus of having committed a grave discourtesy. I considered that better than nothing.

A few days later we were notified that the Washington Square Bookshop had been served with papers by the Society for the Suppression of Vice for having sold a copy of the *Little Review* containing Joyce's Episode XIII. The complainant was a man—a father. We came in from Brookhaven to consult John Quinn.

What did I tell you? raged Quinn. You're damned fools trying to get away with such a thing as "Ulysses" in this puritan-ridden country. (His sixteen-hundred-dollar endowment had been primarily to assure our publishing "Ulysses.") I don't think anything can be done. I'd fight it for you, but it's a lost cause. You're idiots, both of you.

I suggested mildly that we would get someone else to fight the case, knowing that no power on earth could have wrested that privilege from him.

No, I'll see what can be done. But remember I'm doing it for Joyce, not for you. It's too bad you two are mixed up in this thing. You haven't got an ounce of sense.

One didn't argue with John Quinn. One enjoyed his performances too much. He was better than a prima donna. No woman would throw such obvious scenes, or look around so hopefully for the applause of her audience. By our next interview he had decided that he could do a great deal. For one thing he could put the government in its place. His secretaries and office boys were invited in to hear his predictions. I told him I would rather spend an hour in his office listening to him talk than go to the best matinée in New York. This so pleased him that he called in the rest of the office force.

There were moments when we didn't get on with John

Quinn as gracefully as this—moments when Ezra Pound was anxious about our relations.

Tell Jane not to cheek Quinn, Ezra once wrote—to our bewilderment, since Jane had always been careful to appear innocuous. He's no fool. I've seen him go through a pile of Augustus John's drawings, picking out the best without hesitation and with the eye of an expert.

It is true that John Quinn had a passion for "going through" things. He once went through a copy of Sherwood Anderson's "Poor White," meticulously correcting every grammatical error. After which he sent it to Sherwood with words of advice on how to avoid similar errors in a forthcoming work. I don't know if Ezra would consider this a sign of intelligence, but he was always defending Quinn:

Chère M.,

ALL right!

ONLY don't go wrong about Quinn. Quinn made me mad the first time I saw him (1910). I came back on him four years later, and since then I have spent a good deal of his money. His name does NOT spell Tight-Wad. The £150 is my figure, NOT his.

I am not looking for a soft job, at least not in that way. Quinn is not a rich man in the American sense of the word. He has what he makes month by month, and most of it goes to the arts. I know part of what he does, and I know somewhat of how he does it. . . . Quinn wanted me to take £120 a year for myself in connection with the Egoist a year or so ago.

The point is that if I accept more than I *need* I at once become a sponger, and I at once lose my integrity. By doing the job for the absolute minimum I remain respectable and when I see something I want I can ask for it. I mean to say, as things stand I can ask for money when Joyce finishes his next novel, or if Hueffer ever gets his *real* book finished.

If I began by blowing 5000 dollars and did no more than I shall now do with 750 I should feel a mucker and there would be nothing ahead.

My whole position and the whole backing up of my statement that the artist is "almost" independent goes with doing the thing as nearly as possible without "money."

I think also Quinn may know more than you think. He works very hard and I think rather excitedly and his talk after hours may not have the precision a sentence would have if a man had nothing to do but write art criticism, and if he took a day to a paragraph.

At any rate, take a bit more time before you finally make up your mind. I wish there were one or two more like him.

I don't know whether his talk about art is like all American talk about art, but his *act* about art is a damn sight different.

Dont insist on his toning down his enthusiasms to a given foot rule.

Old Yeats (J.B.) describes Q. as "the kindest, most generous, most irascible" of men. I have never known anyone worth a damn who wasn't irascible.

Quinn says a number of nice things about both of you, and admires your courage and nerve and energy. This is not a grouch but a prayer . . . I dont believe anybody else will do half or a tenth as much for us, or give us so many chances to make good after a slip.

. . . The other thing is not to let J. H. cheek Quinn too much. I think he likes you both. But still I think it would be better if YOU saw him, than that she should. If they meet, whatever she may think of his artistic judgment, do let her remember that some of the best living artists think a great deal of it. NOT merely because he buys their stuff.

Before the trial we had a preliminary skirmish or two with John Sumner (head of the Society for the Suppression of Vice)—one in the Jefferson Street Police Court and one walking along Eighth Street where he and I engaged in such a passionate exchange of ideas that we had to go into the Washington Square Bookshop to finish. I was embarrassed by the antipathy with which everyone in the bookshop regarded him. He was probably hurt by it and used to this hurt. I found him charming. Certainly he had a number of qualities to recommend him to my interest. He was shy and sensitive and he believed in his ideas as intensely as I did in mine. He loved to talk. He was full of quotations from Victor Hugo and other second-rate minds. He had been brought up this way and there was in his arguments a half-acknowledged eagerness to be convinced that he was wrong. He was the perfect enemy—I won every point and he seemed to like it. He shook his head helplessly when he couldn't find an adequate comeback. People are childish in their attitude toward John Sumner. All their attacks leave him feverishly convinced that he is right. No one attacks his ideas. If I had had time I would have invited him to tea every day for a month, so that we might have got down seriously to an abstract discussion of ideas. I am willing to wager that at the end of the month he would have become as fanatical about a new set of ideas as he still is about his present set.

There is nothing more antagonistic to me than inhumanity—by which I mean in this case the intellectual's method of dealing with a problem like John Sumner—calling names and ignoring the fact that all human beings are alike in their susceptibility to influence, that we all exist by influence alone. It would be the easiest thing in the world to capture John Sumner's mental imagination and set it to work under the magnetic influence of ideas more hardy than his own.

We came to trial before the Court of Special Sessions—a fact in itself which enraged John Quinn. He began his remarks to the judges by protesting against this. Such lack of tact helped him considerably to lose the case.

There were three presiding judges—two with white hair who slept during the major part of the proceedings and a younger man, a Norwegian. Two years later Jane met him at a party.

Why on earth didn't someone tell me you were Norwegian? he asked. I could have changed that verdict for you.

John Quinn's idea was for Jane and me to remain inconspicuous, meek and silent, and to surround ourselves with "window trimmings"—meaning a group of conservative quietly-dressed women and innocent boarding-school girls. We felt that he was wrong in not wanting us to speak. I still believe we could have given a clearer idea of Joyce's motives than he succeeded in doing. He was

219

brilliant in defining Joyce's prestige in the world of letters, in exploiting his own prestige in the legal world, and in scoring government officials whose ignorance didn't permit them to distinguish between literature and pornography. But he didn't stress the quality of Joyce's mind or the psychology which explains Rabelaisian tendencies. When one of the judges protested that he wasn't interested in hearing anything about James Joyce, that he merely wanted to discuss the obscene writing in question, John Quinn let his opportunity slip entirely—without even seeing it, I believe. I nearly rose from my seat to cry out that the only issue under consideration was the kind of person James Joyce was, that the determining factor in æsthetic and moral judgment was always the personal element, that obscenity *per se* doesn't exist. But, having promised, I sat still.

Quinn had decided to use three witnesses to establish the *Little Review's* standing—Scofield Thayer, editor of the *Dial*, Phillip Moeller of the Theatre Guild, and John Cowper Powys. Phillip Moeller was the first to be called and tried to analyze "Ulysses" for the court by explaining the Freudian manner of unveiling the subconscious mind. One of the judges laughed and asked him to speak in a language that the court could understand. Scofield Thayer was forced to admit that if he had had the desire to publish "Ulysses" he would have consulted a lawyer first—and not published it. John Cowper Powys declared that he considered it a beautiful piece of work in no way capable of corrupting the minds of young girls. At this point

Jane longed to get up and explain that if there was anything in the world she feared it was the mind of the young girl.

It then became a question of the specific obscene passages. The prosecuting attorney announced his intention of having them read aloud. One of the sleepers awoke and, regarding me with a protective paternity, refused to allow the obscenity to be read in my hearing.

But she is the publisher, said John Quinn, smiling.

I am sure she didn't know the significance of what she was publishing, responded the judge, continuing to regard me with tenderness and suffering.

Mr. Sumner was asked if he had had other complaints against us and our magazine.

Not at all, he said gallantly, hiding the copies of the five other suppressed issues which he had brought to court with him.

The verdict was inevitably against us. We were fined a hundred dollars (paid by the lady from Chicago who detested "Ulysses") and in spite of John Quinn's furious remonstrances led off to have our finger-prints taken.

I had been docile during the trial but I decided that having my finger-prints taken was my opportunity to make as much trouble as possible.

We were led through many corridors by an Irish policeman, passing John Sumner who was standing at some distance. He raised his hat high in the air as a tribute and an adieu. We entered a small room where several men were in attendance. If they had imagined that registering my digits was going to be a simple matter they were quickly disillusioned. I examined the thick fluid into which I was supposed to dip my well-kept fingers and insisted upon elaborate advance preparations to guarantee its removal. They hadn't enough towels to reassure me. They rushed out to find more. I didn't like their soap. They produced another kind. I insisted on a nail brush. This gave them more difficulty but they found one. Then I managed to make them suffer for my indignity until they were all in a state bordering on personal guilt. I finally offered my fingers with the distaste of a cat and it became their responsibility to convince me that there would be no permanent disfigurement.

And now for God's sake, said John Quinn, don't publish any more obscene literature.

How am I to know when it's obscene?

I'm sure *I* don't know. But don't do it.

*   *   *   *   *   *

John Quinn's letters were full of temperament:

Dear Miss Anderson,

I'm glad that Frank Harris liked Pound's last. Poor Harris! He is more or less a tragic figure but he has an unhappy genius for getting on the wrong side of things.

People differ in their opinions about art as much as they do about literature. People who don't know anything about art and have no feeling for it, still "know what they like." Perhaps there is more dogmatism in regard to writing than there is about painting or sculpture. People think that because they can read and know the meaning of words that they are capable of judging art in words, which is rather a big assumption. While therefore I recognize that there is no absolute standard in regard to what is or what is not art, I can't help but feel that the illustrations in the May number, to which Judge Lamar referred, were not good art or vigorous art and were very feeble things, not worthy of the literary contents of the *Review*, not worthy of publication in any review, and it was, in my opinion, almost an artistic misdemeanor to include them in the *Review*. I don't want to commit a technical libel on the artist by referring to his or her drawings as artistic misdemeanors. Therefore I hasten to add that I am speaking metaphorically and not legally, and that other people may think that they are artistic creations or divine productions. Some people may be built that way. J. Q.

Dear Miss Anderson,

With this I send you a copy of the memorandum which to-day I am sending to Judge Lamar. I have done the best I could in the time that I had to do it in, for I was in Court all day yesterday and was very driven.

I am quite prepared, in advance, for your dissent from my argument both in substance and in form, for I remember, with considerable amusement, your dissenting from my brief in regard to that October number of the *Little Review* which contained the Wyndham Lewis short story. I thought that my brief in that case was about as good a piece of legal reasoning as I had ever submitted to a Court, for I took the only possible line on which a Court could have decided in your favor, namely, that the story made vice unattractive and contained a moral warning. Your line of argument, which appeared in a later number, might have satisfied Nietzsche, namely, that life is a contest and a struggle, and that if in the struggle of the sexes a woman goes down, that merely proves that she is weak and not able to survive, and if she is not strong enough to survive she ought to go down. Biologically considered, your article may have had some reason in it. Ethically considered, it struck me as cruel and unfeeling.

So I am prepared for your condemnation of what you may call my unnecessary apology for Joyce. A defiance of a court or an official may be a very fine thing, but, after all, the verdict is the thing, and I am not in the defy business but the law business. When one is disposed to defy, one should, it seems to me, consider the nature of the person to be defied. And, frankly, the ordinary Government official or Judge is not the sort of person that would interest me very much to defy. It is much more interesting to me to get a favorable decision from him than it is to defy him and lose the case.

Dear Miss Anderson,

You write that you did not dissent from my legal reasoning but only "from the general abstractions that you are always at war with, such as those in my letter of the 14, for instance." It seems to me that your statement that "the design of life can never be called brutal except when it is regarded sentimentally" is very much of an abstraction. Also your statement that "to the artist destruction is as much the order of the universe as creation" seems to me to be very much of an abstraction and to be quite unsupported by the facts. Destruction may be "the order of the universe" in the natural world, but one could hardly call the Chinese, Hindoo, Egyptian, Persian, Greek and Roman builders destroyers; nor the Greek dramatists and poets; nor

224

the builders of the Christian cathedrals; nor Shakespeare, nor the great musicians whom you love so much.

Again your statement that you "can't think of life in any terms except of design" seems to me to be nothing but an abstraction.

Your allusion further on in your letter to my "valiant defense of Joyce" is not an abstraction, and it pleased me very much. Without employing any abstraction I want to say that I was pleased at what you wrote about my defense of Joyce, the more so as clients are as a rule too stupid to understand what a lawyer does for them and too insensitive to know how to thank a man.

I cordially agree with you in your protest that "merely normal functioning should never be called vice." Vice and sin might be claimed to have been invented by priests. It perhaps would not be equally fair to say that chastity was invented by women, or that, as Bismarck said about Italy, if it didn't exist it would have to be invented. Somehow continence and chastity seem to bracket themselves with vice and sin. I am in quite cordial agreement with you also about an act in which "the woman participates equally with the man." The only qualification I would make would be that so often women do get the worst end of it. That is why, though votes for women is an absurdity in itself, it will be a good thing for women, even though they do add an element of hysteria to public consideration of questions. They could hardly do worse than many of the men who have bungled things.

I should like to see Mrs. Pankhurst the First Lord, or Lady, of the British Admiralty. If she had been in command at Jutland she would not have jellicoed the battle. She would have gone into it to a finish and the war might have ended a year or two earlier, for with the German Navy destroyed the German ports could have been blockaded and submarine warfare would have been made impossible. She has more brains than Sir Eric

Geddes, the he-Lady of the Admiralty, beef down to the hoof, and she would not have trusted the Germans in the possession of the surrendered fleet at Scapa which ought to be called Scapa-up-the-Flue. By the way, Jellico's official title is, I think, Viscount Jellico of Scapa. He left off the "Flow," but he should now add "up-the-Flue."

During the trial and afterward not one New York newspaper came to our defense, not one spoke out for Joyce, not one cared to be identified with the "Ulysses" scandal.

I'm disappointed in you, said Mary Garden. I thought you'd go to jail.

I shared her disappointment. It is always a mistake to allow the persuasions of your friends or your lawyer to keep you out of jail. If I had refused to permit the payment of the fine I might have circulated some intelligent propaganda about "Ulysses" from my cell. Still I suppose the *New York Times* and the others would have refused to give it space. It was not until much later when Sylvia Beach published "Ulysses" in book form in Paris that our three-year propaganda began to have its effect. The *New York Times* must have astonished its readers when finally it began to devote columns to James Joyce's masterpiece.

From then on books of criticism appeared every week lauding "Ulysses," interpreting it for the general public, often misunderstanding it, and always omitting to mention in spite of our copyright and our trial that it had first been published in the *Little Review*.

* * * * * *

Our endowment fund had lasted the better part of a year but now we were penniless again. I went to see Otto Kahn, hoping that he would help.

Yes, he said, some intelligent help ought to be arranged for the *Little Review*. I'll come up and talk with you both about it.

He came to see us in Eighth Street, admired the magenta floor and the black walls (against which his yellow tea rose boutonnière was effective) and talked with genius about the *Little Review's* financial problems. He made a summary of ten points which covered the ground.

I'm interested in your personalities, he said. Do you exploit them sufficiently? Do you go about a lot?

I answered that one can't go about comfortably without being well dressed.

Yes, of course. I should say the *Little Review* needs about four thousand dollars to start with. That will remove your worries about the publication end of it and provide a few pretty dresses.

Wonderful! I said. Then we can go everywhere. And we can talk everywhere. We really can make most interesting talk.

Oh, no one wants to hear any talk, he said looking amused. Just go about. Let people see the color of your eyes and your hair and the way you wear your clothes.

227

No one cares about anything else nowadays. Of course your 'Ulysses' affair was badly managed. John Quinn is rather old-fashioned, I'm afraid. I should have given you Morris Gest as a publicity agent and had the case on all the front pages. That would have helped you.

Yes, that would have helped. So would have the promised four thousand dollars which for a reason we have never been able to explain did not materialize. I had tea with Otto Kahn once or twice after his visit, and found him charming and interesting. We talked of the four thousand dollars as a foregone conclusion. Another time I couldn't go to tea. Jane and I made plans to use the endowment with super-intelligence but finally we received a letter saying that it would not be forthcoming. Otto Kahn being known as a man of his word, this was an enigma as well as a shock. We discussed all the possible reasons for the disaster, and could find none.

*   *   *   *   *   *

Life began to look dark again. I began to look everywhere for money. I interviewed rich men who were interested in the arts and tried to persuade them to make up a subsidy for us. Men like Maurice Wertheim would gladly give a hundred dollars, but it was impossible to amass a fund. We touched bottom again. I could have survived it—but I lost my piano.

New York was not so prodigal of pianos as Chicago or San Francisco. I had a small Mason and Hamlin grand, the rental of which was covered partly by an advertisement, partly by a small monthly payment. The day came when I couldn't make the payment. Several days of that kind came. I wrote the piano company that better days would surely come. But one morning I opened the door to an insistent knocking and a burly man with papers pushed his way past me saying that he had come to take the piano. I thought he must be insane, or that I was. I told him that I couldn't imagine anyone in the world having the courage to talk of taking my piano. He said: it didn't take no courage. I said that if he dared touch my piano I would strike him. I made him sit down while I rang up the piano company. They were sorry, they could do nothing about it. They were short of grands and were calling in all those with unpaid rentals. I promised to find the money instantly. No, they were sorry, they needed the piano. I became angry. The burly man became angry. He pulled the receiver out of my hand.

Say, he shouted, this lady ain't got no respect for law and order. She must be a Bolshevik.

I said: I respect law and order so much that I'll get a policeman in here to preserve it.

I called up the Jefferson Street police court and told them to send a policeman quickly. The burly man, still unsure, went into my room toward the piano. I stood in front of it screaming that I would hurt him if he touched it. The policeman arrived running. He was six feet tall. He looked at the burly man and backed away.

I can't do anything, he apologized, he's higher up than me.

Other men came up the stairs. They were going to take the piano to pieces and let it down on ropes from the window.

I told the policeman to stand by the door anyway—he looked impressive there. I held the others at bay as long as possible until finally they pulled me away and began moving the piano toward the window. Then I had to give up. There was nothing more I could do.

* * * * * *

As we approached the tenth anniversary of the founding of the *Little Review* I felt that we approached its logical conclusion. Jane felt nothing so decisive. I argued that it had begun logically with the inarticulateness of a divine afflatus and should end logically with the epoch's supreme articulation—"Ulysses."

Besides I had never considered that my personal destiny was to be confined within that of the *Little Review*. Ten years of one's life is enough to devote to one idea—unless one has no other ideas. I had several others. By 1922 I knew that I had had enough of one type of struggle. For a number of years life had had the aspect of a polar expedition—all life serving only to maintain life. It was time to change such an existence. It was time to bring the *Little Review* to an end.

But this decision met with a staggering resistance from Jane. She and I had always been at swords' points about theories of personal development. The quality of the L.R., its personality, the thing that set it apart from other maga-

zines of its type, was its reflection of these intense conflicts between its editors.

I believed in freedom and justice. Jane believed in
neither. In her view "all interesting things begin beyond
justice," and as to freedom "there is no such thing—only
the other person is free."

I admitted these views to be worthy of consideration.
I could never find a first-rate refutation of the first, though
I am sure there is one. The second is easily refuted by the
statement that one is interested in the other person's freedom as well as in one's own.

For a long time I had wanted freedom from household
drudgery, from publishing drudgery. I wanted to escape
both by getting a job and supporting the *Little Review*.
Jane considered this going over to the enemy. I tried to
convince her that temperaments opposed on such fundamental questions as justice and freedom should be opposed to living in the same house. They should live their
quite opposed rhythms on opposite sides of the street.
Jane agreed but argued that it was the opposition under
one roof that gave her an incentive to write. Without opposition life would be insipid—without it she would never
write another line for the L.R. This threat kept me
drudging on. It was certainly sufficiently unrelated to justice, but I couldn't see that it was interesting.

I didn't know what to do about life—so I did a nervous
breakdown that lasted many months.

I wrote a dialogue for the L.R. which expressed something of the tension between us:

Dialogue

Scene: *The* Little Review *in ineffectual conversation over the major tragedies of the winter.*

M.C.A. With all the exasperations of contemporary life I seem on the point of losing my interest in things.

jh. Give me a few moments of your exasperated time and we'll get out another of our famous annuals.

M.C.A. Known as the *Little Review?*

jh. Not so largely known. . . .

> *(atmosphere of concentrated impotence)*

M.C.A. We must act!

jh. I see a great deal of action all over the place.

M.C.A. You must create!

jh. I know of no commandment to create.

M.C.A. You might do something if you weren't so neurotic.

jh. Since when have the unneurotic been so creative?

M.C.A. If we didn't waste so much time in good conversation we might at least be self-supporting.

jh. Be self-supporting—and take the conversation that goes with it.

M.C.A. Well . . . it might be called an impasse . . . but thank heaven I can still get some ecstasy out of life.

jh. Why limit me to ecstasy?

I loved the last line. But I also loved ecstasy. It is well to know your own limitations. For years I would probably not enter that cycle of life in which one puts away childish things. Ecstasy is the best prelude to development—just as Blake was right in calling excess the road to wisdom. It might be five years before I would become an interesting person—that is, one who has emerged from her adolescent admirations. Those years I meant to spend in my congenital lyricism. Cleaning the house and addressing envelopes no longer left me feeling unconquerably lyric. People had always said I looked as if I were on a secret errand.

(What do you mean—secret, laughed Jane.)

But I believed in my errand if not in its obviousness. I also believed in "the broad and ample movement of life." Movement implies change.

Sherwood Anderson came in one day when we were discussing the significance and (to Jane) the insignificance of change.

Change is a fine thing, drawled Sherwood. It's bad to grow static. If you can make a change consciously it's very good. I have never found the courage to do this. I used all the subterfuges of the unconscious; I have found myself lost in the woods after a day and night of wandering simply because I wanted to change the current of my life and didn't know how to do it. The getting lost amounted to a sort of conscious aphasia.

*   *   *   *   *   *

Two events helped me to determine the type of change I wanted. One of them was talking with William Butler Yeats, who came over to visit America. John Quinn was his host in New York.

233

Yeats had been one of our earliest contributors and had continued to send us poems through all the years. He had always represented to me, as poet and therefore as man, "the fragile mighty thing" of his own definition. Meeting him only bore out the impression. What suaveness of life, what indications of a great existence—with "all the imminent and authentic tragedies present"—perhaps a definition of the poignant human being that I seem to have been searching through the pages of this book.

Yeats had many amusing stories to tell of James Joyce and Ezra Pound—of Pound's entrée into and repudiation of the intellectual life of London; of the very young Joyce's first visit to him (Yeats) and the cross-examination to which he was subjected. As they discussed theories of prose and poetry, Joyce's face fell.

Ah, he said to Yeats, it is sad that you have met me too late.

I was so entranced listening to Yeats' stories about the people in Europe I wanted to know that I suddenly found the key to my present discontent.

It was the time to go to Europe.

The second event gave form to the wish. I met Georgette Leblanc (Maeterlinck) and had an opportunity to begin a pianistic career by playing accompaniments for her on a forthcoming European tour.

Georgette Leblanc was having a terrible time in America but finding it a wonderful country. She was seeing the worst of our national characteristics but, in spite of dishonest managers and the Hearst press, finding us an adorable mad race.

She had a mysterious, beautiful and theatrical face, and I was prepared for the theatrical nature that was generally attributed to her. I went to the meeting without much interest. Again I found popular legend absurd—in this case because, as Georgette Leblanc says, of the "disastrous discrepancy between my appearance and my nature." She had been called the tiger woman. But at those times when she was supposed to be devouring men she could be found at home devouring cold carrots prepared by a vague and literary *femme de chambre*; reading the philosophers, writing moral essays, laughing at the infinite amusement of life, and not remarking that the carrots were cold. She talked like St. Just, Maeterlinck had always called her Spinoza, and, like Mary Garden, she would have liked to be a great lawyer. She too had a passion for freedom and justice. Injustice of the most excruciating type—misinterpretation—had given her an authentic tragedy. Her sense of freedom (for the other person) had led her to penury. Legend had given her a broken heart. On the contrary she had a strong heart and a clear head. Her knowledge of human stupidity I found to be comprehensive—which may explain why she never indulges in it. *Hélas*, she says, *jamais le génie n'égalera l'abondance, la continuité, l'imprévu de la bêtise.*

During the summer Allen Tanner and I went to visit

her in Bernardsville, New Jersey, where we were to live exclusively on music. In the entrance hall there was a handwriting on the wall: *"Tout est bien: il suffit d'être maître de soi."*

We had heard that there was a young composer of promise living not far from Bernardsville. One is unoptimistic about young composers of promise, but we decided to invite this one to come to see us. He wrote that it would please him to come if we were interested in modern musics. It was the musics that made us await his appearance with a certain expectancy. His name was George Antheil.

He appeared on a Sunday afternoon, carrying a large suitcase of music. He was short, his nose had been maltreated in an airplane accident, he was unprepossessing except for his vitality and his air of concentration. As we began talking he happened to be sitting across the room from the piano. We asked him to play. He reached the piano in two strides and began to beat upon it a compelling mechanical music.

He played everything he had written up to this point in his life—he was just nineteen as I remember. Then he played every other kind of music, even Chopin, with a mastery and a hardness that were admirable. He played his own transcriptions of "L'Après-midi d'un Faun" and the Stravinsky Berceuse ("L'Oiseau de Feu"). We were impressed with everything he did. His transcriptions alone showed him a master of the mathematics of harmony. He used the piano exclusively as an instrument of

236

percussion, making it sound like a xylophone or a cymballo.

George Antheil's parents were Polish, poor, pleased with his musical ambitions but unable to help him launch himself. Georgette Leblanc invited him to stay with us. He took the invitation so urgently that he rushed away that night and rushed back the next day carrying another large suitcase filled with a few clothes and a great quantity of music paper.

For two months we lived the life of several musical colonies. The piano was practiced on all day. Every night after dinner our formal concert began. There was no monotony in these everings. No two people play with greater diversity than Allen Tanner and George Antheil. I am not among those who care only for percussion so Allen remained my favorite pianist. I suppose there was no page of the world's great music that wasn't played or sung during those two months and several that were repeated every night, principally the Pelléas score with Georgette singing the two rôles. If our food wasn't regular our music was.

George was given a room with eastern windows as he began composing with the rising sun. He kept his room in fanatical order. His work table never held more than a pad of paper, laid straight with the lines of the table, an inkwell, pen and pencil placed with the precision of mechanical music. During those weeks one passed his open door at any moment without discovering the pencil in any but a vertical relation to the paper.

237

By ten in the morning he was at the piano where he composed all day. He set poems of Amy Lowell and Adelaide Crapsey. He composed his first concerto for the piano and orchestra, his "Golden Bird" and the first of his famous Mechanisms.

The days of food shortage did not worry George. He rarely ate anyway—except for frequent imbibings of peppermint which he carried in a small bottle in his vest pocket, and infrequent green apples—when he could find any green enough.

He wrote endless verbose letters to Ernest Bloch who had been his first and only professor. His conversation I found stimulating. I have never known anyone who could change his point of view on every subject everyday and still remain interesting.

*   *   *   *   *   *

George Antheil was ready for Europe before any of us. He advertised for a promoter and found one in Philadelphia—Mrs. Edward Bok. He decided to become a virtuoso within three months. He did. Georgette Leblanc invited people to her New York apartment to hear his first concert before he sailed. The father and mother Antheil were there, too moved to speak.

George went directly to London where he gave a concert before a discriminating audience, including Harold Bauer, but he was too frightened to do his best. He then went on to central Europe where he began to create sensations. I introduced him to Ezra Pound in Paris and

Ezra's book, "Antheil and the Treatise on Harmony," was the result of their meeting.

Allen was the next to go.

I was the next.

I am definitely giving up the *Little Review*, I told Jane.
You can't give it up. You started it.
Are you mad? I started it—I can give it up.
You have no sense of responsibility.
Self-preservation is the first responsibility.
You certainly can't give it up.
I certainly can give it up. I'll give it to you.

(I considered this just—as well as interesting, but Jane stopped saying good morning to me.)

Jane too decided to go to Europe.

*   *   *   *   *   *

Our crossing was eventful—musically. John McCormack was on board, Emilio de Gorgorza, Vladimir Golschmann. Every night we gathered in McCormack's suite where the stars sang until morning. I liked Mc-

Cormack's close-range singing better even than his public concerts. He sat on a chair, close to his accompanist, conducted and sang in exquisite pianissimo.

My god, my god, it's too beautiful, he would exclaim over some phrase of Hugo Wolf, singing it five times in succession.

The Duchesse de Richelieu also wanted to sing. McCormack began a sentimental thing of Chausson, asking Georgette to observe his French diction. The duchesse sang with him. McCormack's treatment of the song saved it from sentimentality and he kept cautioning the duchesse between phrases: Don't exaggerate. As they approached the climax she felt her opportunity had come. She showed signs of swooning on the high note.

In tempo! In tempo! yelled McCormack, conducting with all his might.

She retarded with great feeling in the wrong place and McCormack, white with anger, broke off in the middle of the phrase and shut himself in his bedroom. He stayed there ten minutes and came out still looking white, but composed. There was no more music that night.

I can't stand that kind of thing, he said. Edwin Schneider and I sometimes work eight hours on a single phrase.

He and Georgette Leblanc gave the concert the last night out. Mc.Cormack was so nervous all day that he paced the promenade deck.

I'm always nervous, he explained, even if I'm only going to sing four little songs. Once Gatti-Cazazza asked me to sing at a Christmas matinée at the Metropolitan. Our family Christmas was ruined. My wife says she'll never let me accept another Christmas engagement.

After the concert we had a champagne supper and drank to the eternal glory of France.

I don't understand why Americans are so eager about France, said Georgette. It's a beautiful country, and Paris is the most beautiful of cities if you will. But Americans are a people *en marche*—the French are sitting down.

Nevertheless as the evening ended with requests for poems I noticed that she recited Baudelaire, Verlaine, Rimbaud, Apollinaire, with full appreciation for France's glory.

I didn't know what she meant by "sitting down" until I had been in Paris a week.

PARIS

Le Havre. A May morning.

We were to go by motor to Paris. We took the high road through the first Normandy villages and looking down toward the Seine about half an hour out of Havre, I saw rising from the rocks the most fabulous fairy castle of my experience. If my experience was limited the medieval castle was not.

Yes, said Georgette, hearing my exclamations, that's where my sister lives.

But why didn't you tell me you had a sister in a castle?

Chateau life has never interested me, said Georgette, slightly embarrassed.

I thought of my excessive interest in diminutive ranchhouses, tents, gold rooms, Brookhaven, and felt that here at least it would appear less excessive.

It was in the chateau of Tancarville later in the summer that I first had the time and the perspective to examine my American childhood, adolescence, and late youth and to measure the degree of their tension. Perhaps it would

have been better to have spent some of the time sitting
down.

*   *   *   *   *   *

Jane arrived, and she and I went first to see our foreign
editor Ezra Pound.

He was living in one of those lovely garden studios in
the rue Notre Dames des Champs. He was dressed in the
large velvet beret and flowing tie of the Latin Quarter
artist of the 1830's. He was totally unlike any picture I
had formed of him. Photographs had given no idea of his
height, his robustness, his red blondness—could have
given no indication of his high Rooseveltian voice, his
nervousness, his self-consciousness. After an hour in his
studio I felt that I had been sitting through a human experiment in a behavorist laboratory. Ezra's agitation was
not of the type to which we were accustomed in America
—excitement, pressure, life too high-geared. It gave me
somehow the sensation of watching a large baby perform
its repertoire of physical antics gravely, diffidently, without human responsibility for the performance.

Other characteristics of Ezra's puzzled me and I was
unable to explain them until later. They were the marks
that one finds upon all expatriates who have remained
away for too prolonged intervals perhaps from their native
country. I am the last person to underestimate the evils of
the pressure of contemporary American life—also the last
to underestimate the benefits of contemporary European
existence. But there is no denying that there is something

alive at the American core and that cutting oneself off from it slackens the pulse. Three characteristics mark all confirmed expatriates: (1) slowness on the up-take, (2) the tendency to personalize the impersonal—interpreting in terms of politeness or of policy what should be kept clearly in terms of ideas, (3) the tendency to orientalize one's attitude toward women.

Ezra had become fairly patriarchal in his attitude to women. He kissed them upon the forehead or drew them upon his knee with perfect obliviousness to their distaste for these mannerisms. In fact Ezra ran true to form, as the academic type, in everything—as I had anticipated. I am very fond of Ezra. Only it will be more interesting to know him when he has grown up.

* * * * * *

James Joyce was grown up before he left his twelfth year, I suppose. I don't mean grown up in the sense of living his life consciously. No one of my acquaintance has ever practiced that unique activity. Joyce became a man early in the sense that very early he had defined what his personal situation was to be in respect to his fellow man. His focus on his own particular drama was clearly defined in his mind—the difference that becomes the tragedy.

James Joyce and his wife came to see us in Ezra's studio. Joyce was like a portrait of my father as a young man— the same gentle bearing, the same kindliness, the same deprecating humor in the smile, the same quality of personal aristocracy.

In one respect the meeting was a surprise to me. I had been prepared to see a sensitive man but I immediately felt Joyce's strata of sensitization as beyond any possibility of immediate appraisal. He gave me the impression of having less escape from suffering about irremediable things than anyone I had ever known. It was an impression borne out by nothing that he said so much as by the turn of his head, the droop of his wrist, the quiet tension of his face, his quick half-smile. It is borne out by the irremediable facts he must accept. No writer has such need of his eyes as Joyce—the revision of five or six proofs of his vast books cannot be done by anyone else and would strain a perfect eyesight. And Joyce's eyesight is failing.

James Joyce talks little. He curtails his wit, his epithet, his observation by stopping short in the middle of a pungent phrase and saying:

But I am being unkind.

Sometimes he tells stories like this one:

Some friends were eager that he and Marcel Proust should meet. They arranged a dinner, assured that the two men would have much to say to each other. The host tried to start them off.

I regret that I don't know Mr. Joyce's work, said Proust.

I have never read Mr. Proust, said Joyce.

And that was the extent of their communication.

I have seen no contemporary comment that does justice to Mrs. Joyce. She is charming. She is good drama. Her Irish mockery and personal challenge furnish Joyce with a continual, necessary and delightful foil. She teases and tyrannizes him. There is an undercurrent in her voice that makes her mockery at once exasperating, exciting and tender.

She must be at ease to show her quality. She has a feeling of inferiority before "intellectuals," though she would not mince words in expressing her scorn of them. She was quickly at ease with Jane and me, seeing our appreciation. Norah Joyce is one of those women a man loves forever and hopes one day to take effectively by the throat. She has spirit and independence which she has been willing (one feels not without rebellion) to subordinate to her devotion to a man she considers great in spite of "his necessity to write those books no one can understand."

The Joyce household also comprises a son and daughter whom their parents are enthusiastically manipulating into a singer and a dancer. But the interest of the family is clearly focused in the older generation.

Our talk that first evening at Ezra's was disappointing. It was one of those gatherings of people who have a great deal to say to each other, in which the very interest of the things to be said imposes a doubt in advance that they can or will be said. Fortunately there were other evenings in which we all achieved a measure of being ourselves, especially when the wine helped Joyce to tell of his curious telepathic experiences in putting real life into his stories so that people often wrote asking how he dared expose their personal tragedies; and Norah begged him to "come home now or you'll be talking and feeling too much and who'll be taking care of you to-morrow?"

As we left Ezra's Joyce asked us to dine with them the next night. A look of distress crossed his face.

I'm afraid it will have to be in a restaurant. We are leaving soon for the summer and the portraits of my family have been taken down from the dining room.

He was deeply troubled by the lack of an ancestral background for dinner. We assured him that it would not derange us seriously.

We dined with the Joyces *en famille*. They were living in an apartment overlooking the Trocadero. It was not large enough to house Joyce's notebooks. He was working at a great disadvantage, having had to leave most of his library and trunks of notes in Italy. His weary way of referring to the notebooks made a tragedy.

The domesticity of the household was reduced to a minimum by the Joyces' custom of addressing the servant in Italian and using this language among themselves for all incidental conversation of the put-on-your-coat-if-you're-going-out-or-you'll-catch-cold type. This cleared away the underbrush and left space for continuity of talk.

Though I rarely try to talk any more, said Joyce, I have been too wearied by people asking me to have some more soup in the midst of conversation. I have come to feel that sustained conversation is impossible. In my books I have my revenge.

Joyce doesn't consider it a valid excuse for people to say they can't read him because he is too hard to understand. When he was a young man he wanted to read Ibsen—wanted it so much that he learned Norwegian in order to read him in the original. He feels that people can make the same effort to read him. He sees no reason why he should make it easier for them.

Joyce was already working on a book which since 1927 has been running serially in *Transition* under the title of Work in Progress. It is now (1930) half finished. In 1923 he could not yet talk of it—to talk put him off the writing. But later he read certain passages to me. One of the most beautiful was the episode of the Dublin women washing clothes in the river, a stone on one bank, a tree on the other, the names of six hundred rivers flowing through the text, the feeling of all life flowing through the women's hands with the water.

Next we went to see Gertrude Stein.

She was living and still lives in the rue de Fleurus in Montparnasse. Her living room, with its Picassos, Braques, Juan Gris, Cézannes, is on the ground floor. The door opens directly from the court, showing a wood fire at the far end and the famous pictures covering the entire wall space.

Gertrude Stein to-day is noted for her hospitality, her

laughter, her clothes, her comfortable talk, as well as for her "incomprehensible" literature and her acumen in buying the modern painters before they became old masters. Since Sherwood Anderson introduced her to American readers her first legend as a decadent æsthete has evaporated in view of the facts. The circulation of a single photograph of Gertrude Stein was strong enough evidence to the contrary. She is now known to be a healthy, robust, amusing woman who dresses in brilliant flowered chintz, heavy men's shoes, drives a battered Ford to her farm and likes to sit about swapping talk with the garage man before she composes addresses to the students of Oxford.

I've been reading the memoirs of certain American congressmen, she told me. Good prose, by the way.

She is convinced that the incomprehensibility of her own prose is a thing of the past.

There is of course no one now who has any difficulty in reading me, she said, adding that she meant anyone of the younger generation.

I for one still have difficulty, a difficulty that is often unrewarded by understanding. And my understanding is often unrewarded by interest.

To me Gertrude Stein's style can be regarded as having two aspects. She has (1) a way of saying things which presents perfectly her special matter; she has (2) a way of repeating those things which detracts from her special manner.

I like it when she says " a woman who had not any kind

of an important feeling to herself inside her." This seems to me interesting and important material. But when, in a book of six hundred thousand words like "The Making of Americans," she repeats this description every time the character appears—which is probably six hundred times —I find the system uninteresting. I don't deny that it gives weight, but to me it is the weight of boredom. Nor do I deny that the weight of boredom has something to do with success. While one can't claim success for Gertrude Stein with the mob, she has an undisputed success with the intellectuals. I suppose no intellectual ever denied her. But all audiences—popular or intellectual—follow the same laws. To be profoundly impressed they must be subjected, somewhere, to the element of boredom.

Take the case of a lecturer. If a lecturer goes slowly and repeats himself and says the same thing in different ways but many times over he shows he has an important feeling to himself inside him, and those who listen feel that important feeling he has to himself inside him and they are not bored, but say he is a lecturer with important being in him. But if he is a quick man and quick to tell his thinking, those who listen feel he cannot have important being in him because he has said things without taking time to think. And if he had taken years to think them and said them then quickly and with care not to take years to say them, no one will feel he has any kind of important feeling to himself inside him and they will say he has light being in him. And it is the same in living. If anyone has a delicate and quick way of living it is always not so

250

important to people as if he had a strong and heavy way of saying.

In other words, people with heavy physical vibrations rule the world.

I defy anyone to say that "The Making of Americans" wouldn't be just as good (much better) if every psychologically descriptive phrase were said once and once only. But if I do not rate Gertrude Stein as high as some contemporary critics do, it is for a more fundamental reason than my lack of enthusiasm for her house-that-Jack-built style. I feel a limitation to the "vital singularity" she is capable of being interested in. I feel this from my conversations with her, from her books. I feel she is full of homely important knowledge of simple vital people, lack of knowledge of many of the human masks, and I am not at all convinced that her imagination would respond to even a preliminary examination of what I would call significant singularity.

In 1922 the *Little Review* had published a Brancusi number.

Constantin Brancusi lives in a stone studio in the Impasse Ronsin, rue de Vaugirard. His hair and beard are white, his long working-man's blouse is white, his stone benches and large round table are white, the sculptor's dust that covers everything is white, his Bird in white marble stands on a high pedestal against the windows, a large white magnolia can always be seen on the white table. At one time he had a white dog and a white rooster. On the stone benches are two cushions, one yellow, the other cerise. With the exception of those cotton cushions all the other material in the studio is wood, stone, metal or marble.

Brancusi came from Roumania where as a younger man Queen Marie wanted him to become a sculptor in the Greek manner. He left for Paris. The soft white statues of the Louvre made him sea-sick. He felt he could relieve his nausea only by casting the Venuses into the Seine.

For a time he cut for Rodin but he couldn't stand this long. For years he worked alone, unknown, and without any thought of selling his work. Since America helped to establish him as the world's greatest sculptor he has sold enough to live in comfort. He is better known to the public in America than in France but this is because the American public is more eager about art personalities than the French. The only statue of Brancusi's visible as a monument in Paris is the Kiss in the Montparnasse cemetery.

A party chez Brancusi is not to be missed. His parties never vary whether they are given for a princess, the Roumanian ambassador, his special cronies Fernand Léger, Marcel Duchamp, Tristan Tzara, the late Eric Satie, or the American influx. He begins his preparations in the morning. Lighting a freshly-rolled cigarette, he strolls out into the rue de Vaugirard and does his marketing. By the time the cigarette is finished he has acquired a chicken, potatoes and a salad. He strolls back to the studio and sculpts until dinner time. When his guests arrive he lays out plates, silver, white paper napkins, wine and champagne glasses, on the stone table. While he laughs and talks with you he makes chicken soup on the clay stove he built himself. When you have finished the soup he grills the chicken over the coals. He fills your glasses constantly, tells stories constantly. Anything will start him off. I put a cigarette in my holder and hesitated to light it until it was placed straight.

Can't you smoke it if it's crooked? asked Brancusi.

With less pleasure, I said.

C'est une idée comme une autre, said Brancusi. You know the story of the man with the long beard. One night at dinner someone asked him how he slept with it— whether he put it outside the bed covers or underneath them. The man had never thought what he did with it. When he got home he experimented to find out. He couldn't decide. He was uncomfortable both ways. He had to cut it off.

Brancusi laughs so hard at this that the tears run down his cheeks. So do you.

After dinner he brings out his coffee machine, grinds and makes a thick black Turkish coffee. Then someone always asks if he will sing and play his violin.

Oh, we will see—later. *Si tout marche bien.*

By which he means if everyone is completely relaxed and at home. Since everyone always is, he brings out the violin and plays folk songs with Roumanian abandon

253

and the smile of a child. He sings to you in a soft timid laughing voice. He dances in his heavy sabots. He produces a small drum and makes Duchamp beat it. He dances wildly on the stone floor. Léger sits with his head on one hand and with the other beats the rhythms on the stone table. He always looks lonely. A young Dadaist (this being 1923) declaims his opinions. Léger looks at him patiently.

I agree with you, he says, bringing down his fist on the table. I agreed with you fifteen years ago.

Tzara talks about the abstract heart and sings to please Brancusi. Duchamp smiles obligingly at everything that is said, whether it is funny or not.

At midnight Brancusi decides to take flashlights. He becomes instantly as serious as if he were beginning a piece of sculpture. He spends an hour adjusting his apparatus to suit him and in examining his audience with a view to good lighting. He seats himself with the group and by an arrangement of long cords takes the picture so as to include himself.

By one in the morning he decides that the night will be lost unless the party will spend it with him in the streets of Paris. Tzara suggests going to the Opera to tear down the statues and put up Brancusis in their places.

Paris will be surprised in the morning, and happier, he says.

Brancusi leads the way through the streets. He stops at cafés where there is music, talks with everyone, drinks with everyone, dances in the middle of the floor. He is not in the least drunk. He is happy.

By seven o'clock in the morning he has led you to the Bois. He lies down flat on the wet grass by the lake with the intention of catching a duck and taking it home to roast. He suggests taking a boat down the Seine to Rouen. Everyone refuses this. So he takes you instead to the Halles for onion soup.

Francis Picabia had become French editor of the *Little Review* in 1922 but we had never had anything from him except a Picabia number. Long before this we had printed Louis Aragon, André Breton, Philippe Soupault, Paul Morand. In 1923-4 we printed the younger Frenchmen— René Crevel, Paul Eluard, Jacques Baron, Joseph Delteil, Tristan Tzara, Drieu de la Rochelle, Pierre Reverdy. We went to see them all in the spring of 1923.

We took George Antheil to the Picabias. They had invited the young French writers, painters and composers to hear him play, and one of the older musicians whom every young musician in Paris loved—Eric Satie. As everyone knows, Satie was a spectacled little man with an umbrella and the air of a bourgeois de province. Everyone knows the story he told of his youth—how bored he was by people saying: Wait until you're fifty—you'll see.

The day of his fiftieth birthday arrived.

I am now fifty, said Satie. I have seen nothing.

The first time I saw Satie he was entertaining a group

of people, keeping them in continuous laughter by making one *mot* after another. Darius Milhaud offered him a chair. It happened to be an extremely ugly and pretentious chair, painted in hideous bright colors. Before seating himself in it he looked at Milhaud in alarm.

What if it should move . . . ?

I asked him for an article about Les Six (Milhaud, Poulenc, Auric, Honneger, Germaine Talieferro, curious, I can't find anyone in Paris who knows what the sixth name was*) for the *Little Review*.

How long an article do you want? he asked.

As long as you like.

Ah, no, he said, disappointed. *Ce sont les limites que j'adore.*

May, 1923, was one of those springs when everyone was in Paris. Or perhaps this is what happens in Paris every spring.

The Swedish Ballet gave nightly galas in the Théâtre des Champs Elysées. Jean Cocteau's Les Mariés de la Tour Eiffel was given for the first time, with costumes by Jean Victor Hugo. Groups of insurgent artists prayed for scandal, hissing, booing, blowing on keys. Cocteau came in with his high hair, his unique hands and his woolen mittens. After a ballet Satie and Picabia appeared on the stage in a motor car to acknowledge applause. They re-

---

*(In New York the sixth name was found to be Jean Cocteau.—Ed.)

ceived enough hisses to please any Parisian. Stravinsky gave his Noces with the Ballets Russes. Milhaud, Auric, Poulenc and Marcelle Meyer played the four pianos. George Antheil contended that Stravinsky stole the four-piano idea from him in Germany the previous year. The Ballets Russes had a new curtain by Picasso—two running women a hundred times larger than life. Picasso sat in Diagaleff's loge, determined to be seen without evening clothes. Braque threatened to hold up a performance —one of his greens had been tampered with. (Braque is the world's handsomest painter.) Satie was discovered in tears because his ballet (décor by Picasso) was applauded less than others. James Joyce was discovered at all the symphony concerts—no matter how bad. Juan Gris was making beautiful dolls. Gertrude Stein was buying André Masson. Man Ray was photographing pins and combs, sieves and shoe-trees. Fernand Léger was beginning his cubist cinema, Ballet Mécanique, with music by Antheil. The Boeuf-sur-le-Toit (named by Cocteau) had a negro saxophonist, and Milhaud and Jean Weiner were beginning their worship of American jazz. The Comte de Beaumont presented his Soirées de Paris, including Cocteau's Roméo et Juliette with Yvonne George. The Dadaists gave performances at the Théâtre Michel where the rioting was so successful that André Breton broke Tzara's arm. Ezra Pound made an opera of Villon's poetry and had it sung in the old Salle Pleyel (where Chopin fainted long ago).

Yes, everyone was in Paris that wonderful spring.

Ernest Hemingway was living in a small apartment on the Left Bank with his very pretty first wife and his extraordinary first baby. Hemingway had trained the baby in coördination by teaching it to thrust out its hand and catch passing flies.

Jane Heap and I went to dine with them and Hemingway read us a story. It was one of the first stories he had written—he had not yet found a publisher. I took it immediately for the *Little Review* and it was brought out later in his first collection, "In Our Time." A few months after his first appearance in the *Little Review* we printed the second story of his to be accepted anywhere—Mr. and Mrs. Eliot—a gem of a story.

Hemingway—or Hem as he is called by his friends, so that no one knows who is meant by "Ernest"—is so different from his legend that there may be no use trying to show him as he is. People prefer to believe what they heard the first time. The photograph with the smile and the open collar which Dorothy Parker feels may have been a mistake is not the portrait of a man who beats his mother or represents a menace to young women. Unless the laws of physiognomy are still veiled in mystery to the majority of mankind. (They are.) Hemingway is so soft-hearted that it must be as much as he can bear to beat a punching-bag; and he is so afraid of falling often in love that he doesn't go about as blithely as he used to. He knows that falling in love, for him, is the absorbing emotional experience which leaves him no time for eating, sleeping, working, living. As with all one-track organisms it cuts him off completely from any other sensuous activity, and the element of sensuousness in every aspect of life is the foundation of his huge enjoyment in living.

The Author of "A Farewell to Arms" is not irresistible to all women—to most, but not all. There was once one in Paris who refused to succumb.

No, she said, that would be too much to manage. I'm not going to give up a few years of my life to being in love with Hemingway.

So Hem would come to the Select every morning and push through the terrace chairs like a prowling animal with a wound.

Gee, have you seen —— —— about anywhere? he would ask, his eyes blank with pain

There is even a legend that Hemingway is stingy. This springs no doubt from his native generosity. I have never seen him look anything but hurt when someone else tried to pay for a dinner, and if the party is supposed to be dutch he becomes violent when the women wish to pay their share.

If I had to choose a single adjective to describe Hemingway I should choose "simple." If it is interesting (and I think it is) to search for people's animal prototypes Jane has found Hemingway's with precision:

Hemingway is a rabbit—white and pink face, soft brown eyes that look at you without blinking. As for his

259

love for boxing and bull-fighting—all that is thrashing up the ground with his hind legs.

"A Farewell to Arms" seems to me the best novel that has come out of America for a long time. It would be an altogether remarkable book if, instead of dealing with a purely accidental instinctive love, it dealt with something a little higher in the scale—say a love experience with some quality of awareness in it. But Hemingway doesn't follow when you tell him this.

I don't get you. Those two people really loved each other. Gee, he was crazy about her.

It will probably be a long time before America will produce any books that deal with the conscious handling of even approximately conscious states of being. America to-day seems to be looking toward the negro as toward a new force. The negro craze is like the alcohol craze. Alcohol isn't a stimulant—it's a release. It is releasing to identify oneself with an easy insouciant amused race. It is not a push up and on.

The American edition of another book came to me in the same post with "A Farewell to Arms." It too is a book about love and war. It too is written by one of the *Little Review* contributors. It is by Richard Aldington and it is called "Death of a Hero."

There is something wrong with this book. Either it is the story of an artist by an artist, or it is the story of a plain man by a plain man. If it is meant to be the former, one cannot reconcile the hero's incapacity to love, to compel love. There has never lived an artist who hasn't been a symbol of love—usually for the love of many people. The women who are supposed to love George Winterbourne are hard dry women, unchanged by their contact with him. His love for them is unmarked by imagination. This is not what happens to the artist in any environment —even in middle-class England.

George does not create his environment, he is created by it. He does not make his experience, he is the victim of his experience. The artist may be regarded as the victim of victims, but at least he never feels that way about it. His illusion may be his limitation—it is certainly his definition. The antagonizing factor about this book, the element that made the critics uncomfortable, is that Aldington is known as a poet and has produced a book that is not a poet's.

If Aldington wanted to debunk the artist's contribution to life he should have told the story of a higher, not a lower, vibration than the artist's.

The two men who have most influenced the young writers of France are André Gide and Jean Cocteau. In 1921 the *Little Review* published Jean Cocteau's long poem, "The Cape of Good Hope," translated remarkably into English by Ezra Pound.

Cocteau is the most charming young man in Paris. All Americans think so, many Parisians think so. Paul Morand is sympathetic, Cocteau is catalytic.

The first time I saw him I had a chance to study his effect on people. He came into a restaurant with two other men. His entrée had the dramatic quality that people of reserve often produce against their will. The holding back of themselves creates a crisis of public curiosity. Cocteau entered with care in every movement—a restrained step, his arms held meticulously at his sides, his face closed, his eyes judging the dangers of an alien atmosphere. The satellites who followed appeared loose, vague, open, unstated, by contrast. Cocteau chose a table with a modulated gesture of an arm, still holding his body with that air of not trusting the mob which is perhaps the underlying distinction between aristocrats and others. Once seated in the safe presence of two people who knew him, he gave no further thought to the aliens.

For more than an hour I observed the chemistry of the catalytic element at work—an audience completely dominated, taking color uniquely from Cocteau's presence, losing it even in those moments when he gave his attention to the maître d'hôtel. In 1923 those persons who disliked Cocteau, who understood nothing he said or did, admitted that any soirée was ruined the moment he left it.

All photographs of Cocteau are inadequate to explain him. His face is so delicate, so constantly in transition, that only the cinema could register its nuances. His hands are even more expressive than his face. They would be merely grotesque—too long, too veined—except that he uses them like words. With every phrase of his talk

262

their gesture changes. The rhythm of their movement is extraordinary. He wears his coat sleeves short, his cuffs tight and turned back. I have never asked him if he does this intentionally, but anyone who loves hands knows that they are more effectively featured when they emerge from a tightened wrist band.

I imagine Cocteau's enjoyment of life as at the opposite pole from Hemingway's. I can imagine no precipitate movement, no robust or careless participation, but a ceremony as finely ordered as the movements of his hands. As if in contrast to this, his nature is spontaneous, nervous, gay, childlike, expansive—*il se livre*. He demands to be surrounded by affection and understanding. He loves his friends and tells them so every day. He loves even his acquaintances—those for whom and in whom he feels a "sympathy." If you are one of these you are liable to be assured of his affection at any moment. He leaves a note in your hotel *casier* in his illiterate handwriting:

J'ai vu votre nom en passant. Je ne peux pas m'empêcher de vous dire combien je vous aime.

Cocteau is one of those writers whose name is impressed upon his generation not so much by what he writes as by what he is. His novels are brilliant personal expositions but if he hadn't written them his poetry would have been enough. If he had written no poetry his plays would have been enough. If he had written no plays his translations would have been enough. And if he had translated nothing, written nothing, he would still have made a legend. Someone would have discovered him leaning from his window at midnight talking the most witty sur-réalism to stray drunkards clinging about the lamp post below.

The legend of Cocteau is founded on his talk. Like the Greek philosophers, he talks to groups of young men. They gather about him each morning for his eleven o'clock levées. Their talk is not that of æsthetes who hope to draw glamour to their own names by disputing the glamour of great names. There is only one kind of talk that has the power to raise a man's name above his generation. Its subject-matter is interest in great ideas.

André Gide's presence indicated this interest. The first time I saw him—in a train enroute to the Riviera—he was talking. The three men to whom he spoke hung on his words with an attention that thought alone can attract.

When we published Gide in the *Little Review* I imagined him as a young man—at least under forty. This was because I didn't know of his symbolist beginnings and his later evolution. He is now sixty. He is bald, often wears a skull cap and a shawl over his shoulders in the Mallarmé tradition. His eyes are brown, his skin is yellow. When "Si le Grain ne Meurt" was published some years ago the frankness of his confessions shocked certain sections of the French public. The translation of the axiom, "Nature abhors a vacuum," is "La nature a l'horreur du vide." Gide's shocked compatriots turned it into, "La nature a l'horreur du Gide."

During 1924-1927 Jane Heap carried on the *Little Review* in New York as a quarterly when circumstances permitted, as an annual when they didn't.

She made it the American mouthpiece for all the new systems of art that the modern world has produced, from the German expressionists and the Russian constructionists to the French sur-réalistes. She opened a Little Review Gallery at 66 Fifth Avenue where the painting, sculpture, constructions, and machinery of these groups were exhibited. In 1926 she organized an International Theatre Exposition, in which Russian constructivist stage-sets were shown for the first time in America. In 1927 she gave a Machine-Age show—modern art in juxtaposition with engineering and the industrial arts, the first exposition of its kind to be shown anywhere.

During these years I stayed in Europe—chiefly in France and Italy. I wanted to find out what old civilizations, races, countries, climates, landscapes would do for me. In some ways these old things made me a new person.

In the beginning I assumed that I would be regarded in Europe as the same human being I had been in America. I went on living, feeling, fighting in the same way.

France seemed an especially good country to fight in. The French were always fighting. Chauffeurs blew their horns with unrestrained personal animosity. Concierges cried insults. Peasants killed old women for fifty francs. Daughters drowned their mothers in deep wells. Politicians screamed at one another in the senate. The people cursed the nobility and the nobility disdained the people.

I felt I would be permitted to fight in my own small way the conditions that antagonized me. I tried to strike a man beating a horse in the street. He prepared to strike me back. I tried to silence a concierge who roused me from sleep at six by flogging a door-mat under my window. She recommended with maledictions that I go and sleep in my own country. I tried to find out from railway officials when trains left—trains that had left for a hundred years. They were uninformed and resented my resentment. I tried to correct the manners of a guard in the subway and was suddenly surrounded by crowds resembling the French Revolution. I tried to impose protection and politeness for women in France. Women of the French mob tried to mob me for it. Men of the French boulevards tried to follow me and resented my refusal of their chivalry. The nation of chivalry appeared to me at first a nation of brutality and I fought the brutality on every street corner.

In Italy I had a fur coat stolen and the police refused other research than my own trunk and the floor under my bed. I was almost jailed for insisting I hadn't stolen my coat myself. In Germany I fought stolidity. In Spain I fought cruelty. In Belgium I fought stubborness.

Coming back to Paris I fought the lack of a sense of

perfection. Symphony orchestras played out of time, tune, and rhythm. "Perfect!" wrote the critics. I was considered disagreeable for disagreeing. Cinema directors cried "Parfait! Allons-y!" when perfection was still several weeks distant. I was considered ill-mannered for mentioning it—a vulgar American.

I fought this unintelligent impression. I saw no reason why I shouldn't go on fighting everything that was unintelligent. But I saw that this was making me disliked in Europe. I like being disliked by people I designate to dislike me. But I cannot say I like dislike coming in from all sides. Personal vanity prompted me to change.

When a salesman offered me cotton instead of the silk I had asked for I no longer said Is silk cotton?—I said Cotton is more to be desired than silk. I was given a piano for a concert in which two notes refused to sound. When the tuner asked Que voulez-vous? I didn't answer that I wanted them to sound. I said that the concert would evidently sound better in proportion as it sounded less.

I no longer stated any interesting opinions. It is dangerous in France to do more than echo what your friends are saying. This has become the criterion of taste, intelligence, and good breeding.

So I changed. But it was only a superficial change. I held in my furies in order to gain time—which is certainly no way to gain development.

And then something happened which changed me fundamentally.

It happened through a phrase of five words.

In the spring of 1925 (1926?—does it matter?) I went to Fontainebleau. I was sitting at lunch in a chateau garden when a tall Englishman joined our group. There was something about him that caught the attention in a sharp way. His face was keen, kindly, and contained, his manner easy and smiling. But there was more challenge in his presence than I had ever felt in another human being. His name was A. E. Orage.

We talked—he and Jane and I. Orage spoke of Eliot's *Waste Land* and Joyce's *Ulysses* as the two high points of contemporary expression—the artist's statement of the present human bankruptcy. He talked of the artist in general, of his psychology in particular.

A man speaking from the stage, said Orage, usually alters his voice, often speaks in a voice unrelated to his natural manner of speech. Writers undergo something of the same transition in putting themselves into their books. I'd give all of *Ulysses* for the letters Joyce wrote the Swiss government when he lost his luggage in that country. Interesting letters. Joyce really wanted his luggage.

As he talked Orage seemed to be simultaneously performing several other feats—taking a complete inventory of our mental and emotional equipment, forcing us to lay our cards on the table, realizing that we might not enjoy this, courteously turning his back that we might recover our bearings, but directing every phrase of the conversation as toward a preconceived intention and result. I tried to discover the intention and became baffled. I felt such admiration for Orage's expertness, such sudden panic as

268

I reflected it was a faculty I might never possess, that I became slightly hysterical. I wanted to shake Orage and shout: Tell me what it is you know that I don't! Next I wanted to weep, as a token of admiration. Then I decided it would be better to discuss my reactions than to scream or weep. So we did. Orage told of what he had been seeking for all his life, what he had found, what he was working at, what its object was. He made careful distinctions between subjective and objective states of being, the former receiving his taboo. He asked me about my life.

What is your object in playing the piano?

As nearly as I can define it, playing the piano is the logical way to recapture continuously that state of ecstasy without which life is not worth living.

That is not an object, corrected Orage. If you say you are playing the piano to make money or to give concert tours you have named objects.

And then he added the five words that have changed my outlook upon life:

Act, said Orage, don't be acted upon.

I thought about this phrase for many days.

I began reviewing my life in relation to its objectives. I saw no objects, I saw only states.

I saw myself committing many actions, but always after having been acted upon; and always to achieve one of three states—liberty, ecstasy, or peace.

Liberty is not a thing, Orage said, it is an idea. And I could see that it might be classified as a vague idea.

269

My give-me-ecstasy-or-give-me-death attitude was not even an idea.

And my strife for peace had been a conscientious effort toward paralysis.

I saw Orage again. This time he said seven words: Remember you're a pianist, not a piano.

For three years I have been investigating and experimenting with the meaning of these twelve words. I have come to understand something of their scope. I have found out that they penetrate every region of life. I have found out that the quality of every life is determined exclusively by its position in relation to acting or being acted upon. I have had the drastic experience of realizing that my thirty years of fighting have been not actions but reactions.

In 1929, just fifteen years after the *Little Review* had been launched as a magazine in which I could record my reactions I decided that there had been enough of this. Everyone was doing it—the artist above all. The artist organism is preëminently the acted-upon organism.

Jane agreed with me at last that the *Little Review* should be brought to a close.

We began preparations for the final number in Paris. I felt that it would be uninteresting to publish a conventional number, but that it might be stirring to ask the artists of the world what they were thinking and feeling about their lives and work. We drew up a list of simple but essential questions and sent them to all our contributors. The final number of the *Little Review* was composed of the responses we received from more than fifty of the foremost men and women in the arts.

These were the questions:

QUESTIONNAIRE

1. What should you most like to do, to know, to be? (In case you are not satisfied.)
2. Why wouldn't you change places with any other human being?
3. What do you look forward to?
4. What do you fear most from the future?
5. What has been the happiest moment of your life? The unhappiest? (If you care to tell.)
6. What do you consider your weakest characteristics? Your strongest? What do you like most about yourself? Dislike most?
7. What things do you really like? Dislike? (Nature, people, ideas, objects, etc. Answer in a phrase or a page, as you will.)
8. What is your attitude toward art to-day?
9. What is your world view? (Are you a reasonable being in a reasonable scheme?)
10. Why do you go on living?

I regret that we didn't add another:

11. Do you know what has been the motivating force behind every act of your life?

I wrote a farewell editorial stating that I didn't want to hear any more about the artist transforming life. I know he transforms it. But I am not interested at the moment in transformation. I want a little illumination.

Jane wrote a farewell editorial which, judging by the editorial comment it received in the American press, was not widely understood. I take pleasure in quoting it here:

LOST: A RENAISSANCE

I am bringing the Little Review to an end, for my part, because I have found the answers to some of these questions.

It is a matter for speculation whether anyone who has tried to get at real answers would dash into print with the results. I at least am keeping my answers for my own use and enlightenment. Instead, I am going to indicate the difference between the Little Review and other magazines, and try to show that this same difference is carrying us into quite other activities.

The revolution in the arts, begun before the war, heralded a renaissance. The Little Review became an organ of this renaissance. Later magazines, perhaps, had somewhat the same intellectual program, but the Little Review had the corresponding emotions; and consequently an energy that nothing has been able to turn aside . . . except itself.

No doubt all so-called thinking people hoped for a new order after the war. This hope was linked with the fallacy that men learn from experience. Facts prove that we learn no more from our experiences than from our dreams.

For years we offered the Little Review as a trial-track for racers. We hoped to find artists who could run with the great artists of the past or men who could make new records. But you can't get race horses from mules. I do not believe that the conditions of our life can produce men who can give us masterpieces. Masterpieces are not made from chaos. If there is confusion of life there will be confusion of art. This is in no way a criticism of the men who are working in the arts. They can only express what is here to express.

We have given space in the Little Review to 23 new systems of art (all now dead), representing 19 countries. In all of this we have not brought forward anything approaching a masterpiece except the "Ulysses" of Mr. Joyce. "Ulysses" will have to be the masterpiece of this time. But it is too personal, too tortured, too special a document to be a masterpiece in the true sense of the word. It is an intense and elaborate expression of Mr. Joyce's dislike of this time.

Self-expression is not enough; experiment is not enough; the recording of special moments or cases is not enough. All of the arts have broken faith or lost connection with their origin and function. They have ceased to be concerned with the legitimate and permanent material of art.

I have not come to this opinion hastily nor through any habitual pessimism, but only after years of observation, revaluing, and learning. I hold no disappointment, despair, or fears for the future. I hold no negative emotions. The actual situation of art today is not a very important or adult concern (Art is not the highest aim of man); it is interesting only as a pronounced symptom of an ailing and aimless society.

This is the situation as I see it. My "luminous certitude" that it could be changed made of me a victim of the Little Review. In spite of logic, deprivations, financial catastrophies and Mr. Sumner, we have gone on running the Little Review; or I thought I had until I found that it was running me. I was a victim as much as any saint, savant, or business man. But my

273

idea of victimization has been enlarged. It is this that now needs my attention.

I am not going out to try to reform or reorganize the world-mind. Nor am I going to sit and brood about the passing of the arts. The world-mind has to be changed, no doubt; but it's too big a job for art. It is even quite likely that there will have to be reorganization on a very large scale before we can again have any thing approaching great objective art . . . or approaching life.

Perhaps the situation is not so hopeless as I have described it. Perhaps it doesn't matter. Or perhaps it would be more than an intellectual adventure to give up our obsessions about art, hopelessness, and Little Reviews, and take on pursuits more becoming to human beings.

j. h.

I am trying to become a new human being. I still make vows to achieve an increasingly beautiful life. I think of Chicago and the lighthouse sending its searchlight into my window. I no longer look out upon a lighthouse. I live in one.

Tancarville, 1929.   *Paris, 1929.*

INDEX

275

277